Louis Dupont Syle

Essays in Dramatic Criticism

Louis Dupont Syle

Essays in Dramatic Criticism

ISBN/EAN: 9783337345563

Printed in Europe, USA, Canada, Australia, Japan

Cover: Foto ©Thomas Meinert / pixelio.de

More available books at **www.hansebooks.com**

ESSAYS

IN

DRAMATIC CRITICISM

WITH

IMPRESSIONS

OF

SOME MODERN PLAYS

BY

L. DUPONT SYLE

ASSISTANT PROFESSOR OF ENGLISH LITERATURE
IN THE UNIVERSITY OF CALIFORNIA

NEW YORK
WILLIAM R. JENKINS,
851-853 Sixth Avenue.

TO

Mrs. Phebe A. Hearst

WHOSE THOUGHTFUL AND LOVING GENEROSITY

HAS MADE POSSIBLE TO SO MANY

THE ATTAINMENT OF IDEALS

THIS BOOK IS DEDICATED

(BY PERMISSION)

AS A MARK OF APPRECIATION.

*All we have willed or hoped or dreamed of good
  shall exist;
Not its semblance, but itself; no beauty, nor
  good, nor power
Whose voice has gone forth, but each survives
  for the melodist
When eternity affirms the conception of an
  hour.
The high that proved too high, the heroic for
  earth too hard,
The passion that left the ground to lose itself in
  the sky,
Are music sent up to God by the lover and the
  bard;
Enough that He heard it once: we shall hear
  it by-and-by.*
        —B<small>ROWNING</small>.

PREFACE.

We are just beginning to have a drama in the United States: the *Impressions* recorded in the second part of this little book are an attempt to preserve material that may (or may not) be useful to the future historian of that drama.

In the *Essays* of the first part, I have endeavored to deal with questions that have a more permanent interest than have those touched on in the *Impressions*.

About two-thirds of the contents of this book has already appeared, in slightly different shape, in the columns of the *San Francisco Examiner*. I have to thank the Management of that paper for permission to reprint here.

TABLE OF CONTENTS.

I.—ESSAYS.

                                                                        Page.
I. The Influence of Molière Upon Sheridan and Congreve........ 3
II. Is the Actor's Art Unworthy?.. 48
III. Some Essentials of the Actor's Art........................ 58
IV. The Endowed Theatre........... 65
V. The Future of the Drama........ 84

II.—IMPRESSIONS.

I. Shall We Forgive Her? — The Serenade....................... 91
II. A Secret Warrant............... 103
III. Robin Hood...................... 111
IV. The Geisha. — Rip Van Winkle (Opera).—A Gilded Fool....... 116
V. The Cat and the Cherub.—The First Born.—A Gay Deceiver.. 125
VI. Shore Acres...................... 135
VII. Trilby.—The Purser............. 145
VIII. Niobe.—In Old Japan............ 154

I.

ESSAYS.

I.

THE INFLUENCE OF MOLIERE UPON CONGREVE AND SHERIDAN.

If one could acquit Charles I. of the cardinal crime of being a liar, there are many aspects of his character that might be dwelt upon with pleasure. Not the least pleasing among these, is his patronage of the Fine Arts; to Vandyck he gave free apartments in Blackfriars Palace, a pension of £200 a year, knighthood and orders for numerous paintings,—some of which were paid for while others were not; to Ben Jonson he not only continued the Laureateship, a hundred pounds a year and the tierce of Canary granted by James I., but he was also pleased publicly to indicate his interest in the drama by considerable grants of money for Masks, by allowing the Queen to appear in a pastoral comedy and by himself acting a part in Jonson's Mask of *Love's Triumph Through Callipolis* (produced in 1630).

Such facts as these show palpably the intimate connection between the Court and the Theatre,—a connection which, while apparently advantageous to the drama, was, in reality, harmful to its life and growth: for it tended to make that drama a mere recreation for a small aristocratic class and to remove it from close contact with the sympathies of an immense majority of the people. Even before the death of Shakespeare the national life had begun to assume forms which, in the eyes of the Court, were strange, fantastic, contemptible. Yet these were the forms which in the end must and did prevail,—forms which represented, in spite of their outward absurdities, a strong, inner, spiritual life, the life of Puritanism. The dramatists, blinded by their devotion to the Court, were unable to perceive and to acknowledge the purity and virility of Puritan motives; they recognized only the surface ridiculosities and lent their willing aid to expose and to deride what they considered the hypocrisy of a class to whom England owes Hampden and Vane,

Milton and Cromwell. When, therefore, king and parliament abandoned hard words for harder blows, the theatrical profession and all connected with it were relieved from the embarrassment of choosing a side : their side was chosen for them by the stern exigencies of the situation into which they had thrust themselves. *Their* cause was lost even before the king's : he was not executed until 1649 ; ten years before this, theatrical representations had all but ceased and the theatre was legally abolished by the parliamentary statute of 1642. This declared that "while these sad causes and set-times of humiliation do continue, stage plays shall cease and be forborne."

For fourteen years there was hardly a dramatic performance in England ; in 1656 D'Avenant obtained permission to produce a kind of musical dialogue which he described as "after the manner of the Ancients." In 1657 he was allowed to give his *Siege of Rhodes*, which he was careful to designate not as a play, but as "a Representation by the Art of Prospective in Scenes, and the Story Sung in Recitative Music." This marks the beginning of the end of Puritan *régime*, and with the restoration of Charles II. in 1660 the theatres were immediately reopened.

For the twenty years, then, from 1640 to 1660, the acting drama had been practically dead in England. When the curtain fell in the first-mentioned year, there were living not only many actors who had been trained in the school of Burbage, Ben Jonson and Shakespeare, but also some dramatists able to support not unworthily the traditions of the Elizabethan stage. Among these were Webster, Thomas Heywood, Massinger, Field, John Ford and Shirley. When the curtain rose again in 1660, the only one left of this illustrious group was Shirley, and he, poor, old and broken by misfortune, never renewed his connection with the stage during the six years of life that were left to him. This fact, trifling as it may appear, seems to me significant of the complete break in the traditions of the English stage caused by those twenty years of Puritan ascendancy. Moreover, the nation, though it had restored the Stuarts as a political convenience, was still Puritan by a large majority, and the aversion from the stage which had crystalized in the drastic ordinance of 1642, when bishops and actors were classed and abolished together,—this aversion was inherited as a tradition, not only by the children of the men who had humbled kings at Naseby and at Worcester, but also by their children's children unto the generations of to day.

This, then, was the condition of affairs which confronted the would-be dramatists of 1660:—a stage with hardly an actor, a broken tradition of great writers, a nation a majority of whose members regarded the stage as the invention of Beelzebub. Under these circumstances it is not surprising that the dramatic authors turned again for audience to that small and exclusive upper class which had formerly been their patrons, and that they sought models among the writers of that nation which had welcomed the king in his exile and had impressed upon him many traits properly characterized as French. While we have not here to deal specifically with tragedy, it may be noticed in passing that the influence of Corneille and Racine is no less clearly traceable in Dryden than is that of D'ancourt in Vanbrugh and of Molière in Wycherley and Congreve.

Here now it may be proper to describe briefly the character and the environment of that Molière comedy which from the time of that writer down to our own has had so vast an influence upon the comedy of every civilized nation.

In the 17th century, the theatre of France, like that of England, was intimately connected with a Court upon whose favor and patronage it depended for its very existence. While the English people, through the stress and strife of civil war, were pushing forward to the goal of constitutional liberty, France, thanks to Richelieu and Mazarin, seemed not only to have lost sight of this goal, but to have forgotten that such a thing existed. While England gained in one direction, she lost in another: the Fine Arts languished and almost died. While France lost in one direction, she gained in another: the Fine Arts grew and flourished, — and conspicuous among these Arts was the drama.

After twelve years of experience as author, manager and actor in the provinces, Molière was invited to Paris in 1658 through the influence of the Prince de Conti and the Bishop of Valence.

His company was taken under the patronage of Philip, Duke of Anjou, younger brother of Louis XIV. For six years Molière grew steadily in the favor of the King, who, in 1664, stood sponsor to the poet's eldest son. The next year the troupe was distinguished by the title of The King's Comedians, and was granted an annual subvention of 7000 livres; nor in the eight years that were to elapse before his death (1673) did Molière ever lose the friendship and patronage of the King. Without the royal protection some of his most famous works, notably *Tartuffe* and *Le Festin de Pierre*, could never have been performed and would probably never have been written. Yet this patronage was far from being an unmitigated blessing. To please the callow taste of his royal master, Molière was compelled to waste much of his time upon spectacles, ballets and farces quite unworthy of him, and whenever in his plays he touched upon questions of politics he was obliged to abandon the artistic attitude of satirist for the degrading posture of flatterer. A king became to him as a king to Beaumont and Fletcher, a thing to be bowed down to and not to be criticised.

But, royalty apart, the life of Paris furnished Molière an extensive field wherein he might exercise his comic genius. If kings could not be sacrificed to the gaiety of nations, fops and marquises could. Hence the long gallery of exquisitely-painted fine gentlemen, conspicuous among whom hang Dorante, the Marquis de Mascarille and the redoubtable Viscount Jodelet. Fine ladies also are not wanting,—ladies who are witty and amiable like Eliante, witty and heartless like Célimène. At the other end of the social scale we have as foils and critics to their superiors the downright, common-sense servant girl, as in Nicole, Dorine, Toinette, and by their side those schemers in petticoats, Frosine and Claudine. Nor is the middle class unrepresented. Monsieur Jourdain needs but mention to be recognized as a type of that snobbishness to be seen in every wealthy society; while the miser, the rake, the hypocrite, the blue-stocking, have each a play. This enumeration, incomplete as it will be recognized to be, may serve to indicate the range of

Molière's observation. His strength lies, it seems to me, in the depiction of this wide range of character by means of just and appropriate dialogue and by means of situations which, though often repeated and seldom highly dramatic, are nevertheless sufficient for their end. While it cannot be denied that in some of his farces he is exceedingly coarse, in the great majority of his plays the moral tone is pure, noble and elevated. For surface polish he may owe something to the refined paganism which was the practical creed of the Court of Louis XIV., but for the deeper ethical treatment which we find in his plays he must have been indebted to his own serious nature,—"this jester, thoughtful as an apostle," as Voltaire has called him.

Molière's work was completed thirteen years after the English Restoration. Some of the best of it, *L'École des Femmes*, for instance, was in existence as early as 1662. With such a mass of splendid material to draw from, with a King and Court devoted to French literature and French fashions, with a stage cleared of Elizabethan traditions as above described, small wonder is it that the Restoration comedy writers helped themselves bountifully from the banquet afforded by Molière's table. Small wonder is it also, if, lacking the fine discriminating taste of the master of the feast, they mingled courses which he had kept separate. Moreover, whenever they found the viands too delicate for their coarse palate, they did not hesitate to season them with ill-flavored and unsavory condiments mixed to suit their English audiences. This process they often refer to as "strengthening" Molière. To us it seems rather a weakening and debasing of that great writer's materials.

Chief among these dramatic criminals stands Wycherley, who evidently influenced Congreve's early work and who himself shows unmistakable traces of the influence of Molière. Wycherley's *The Country Wife* (written about 1672), takes its main incidents from two plays of Molière's, *L'École des Femmes* and *L'École des Maris*. So ingenious is the plot, so diverting are the incidents of the French author's works, that not even the besmirching hand of Wycherley has rendered it impossible to read with interest his

English version. The extraordinary vitality of the Molière elements is shown by the fact that they still survive in a play recently given by Mr. Daly's company,—*The Country Girl.*

Wycherley's *Plain Dealer* (1674), is a debased and vulgarized version of Molière's *Le Misanthrope,* showing correspondencies in plot and characters as follows :—

Plot. The plot in each play turns upon the misfortunes and humiliations which befall a man sincere and outspoken, placed in a highly artificial and conventionalized society. In each case this man distrusts and rails at everybody in the world save two,—himself and the woman he loves In both plays the interest culminates in the scene where the Misanthrope or the Plain Dealer finds that his mistress is false as the rest of her world. In the sub-plot, Molière relieves this somewhat dark picture with light and delicate touches of healthy sentiment and of pure affection, wherein the tone of high comedy and an organic connection with the main plot are perfectly preserved. In Wycherley, the sub-plot is low comedy and has no more connection with the main plot than have negro dialect stories with literature.

Characters. The Alceste of Molière, a man of high temper and of high character, incapable of an unworthy deed, appears in the Manly of Wycherley as a surly, foul-mouthed wretch capable of actions at which an Iago would have shuddered. Philante, the polished and sensible man of the world, appears as Freeman, whose highest ambition is to mend a broken fortune by a doubtful marriage; Oronte, that deliciously absurd coxcomb, is transformed to the traitor Vernish, aptly described by Manly as a man of such extraordinary merit in villainy that the world and fortune can never desert him; Eliante, cousin to Célimène, appears as Eliza, cousin to Olivia; the scandal-mongering Marquises appear as Novel and Lord Plausible; and lastly, Célimène, whose faults are such as may easily be forgiven to her age and sex, appears as that Olivia whose character may be fitly described by Congreve's couplet—

"Heaven has no rage like love to hatred turned,
Nor hell a fury like a woman scorned."

The further indebtedness of Wycherley to Molière may be traced in the conversation between Manly and Freeman (*Plain Dealer*, I., 1), in the scandal-mongering scene of Act II., where Olivia, like Célimène, leads and outrails the railers, and in the incident of the two letters sent by the heroine to her two foppish admirers. To another play of Molière's, the *Critique de l'École des Femmes*, Wycherley is indebted for that effective scene in the *Plain Dealer* where he criticises his own play, the *Country Wife*.

I have given this somewhat detailed study of Wycherley's borrowings from Molière, as they may serve as a type of the adaptations made by many other English dramatists during the Restoration period. Among those who helped themselves freely and too often in Wycherley's manner may be mentioned Dryden, Vanbrugh, Shadwell, D'Avenant, Sedley, Ravenscroft, Crowne, Betterton, Otway, Mrs. Behn. Most of these writers preceded Congreve, and it is natural that in his first play he should have followed the fashion thus set and that he should have imitated particularly the most prominent comedy writer among those just named, — Wycherley. Every young writer is greatly affected by the literary tone or school popular at the beginning of his career; coarse dialogue and *risqué* situations were all the fashion when Congreve began to write, and this may serve to account for and to palliate the presence of these elements in his earlier work.

Congreve's first play, *The Old Bachelor*, takes its name and its principal character from the type set upon the stage by Molière in his *Misanthrope* and by Wycherley in his *Plain Dealer*. Hartwell approaches nearer to his French prototype than does Manly: he is a man of good heart and a gentleman,—the only one in the play. He has more wit than Alceste and more refinement than Manly. Like Alceste, the misfortunes which befall him come from his trusting too well the woman he loves; he has the sympathy of the audience, as has Alceste and as Manly has *not*. When his difficulties are straightened out we rejoice with him that he is allowed to remain what God and nature had evidently intended him to be,—an old bachelor. In Congreve, then, writing at the age of 22, we see a finer art than in those comedy writers who were his immediate predecessors and his contemporaries, for in them, with rare exceptions, every character is painted black and every side of human nature is equally despicable,—a mistaken method of portrayal of which Molière in his comedies is never guilty. The other characters in *The Old Bachelor* are of narrow range and of purely conventional types, drawn rather from a young man's study of books than from observation of actual life. It may be worth while to notice in passing that the traditional animus of the dramatists against the Puritans comes out strongly in the types of that class introduced into the play,— Fondlewife and the spurious Spintext. Three times in this play Congreve employs that weakest of dramatic devices, the Soliloquy. This is a marked feature of Molière's early style, noticeably in *L'Étourdi* and in *Le Dépit Amoureux*. Molière himself, so far as I know, never took the trouble to defend the Soliloquy; Congreve has seen its weakness and has made as good a defense for it as has ever been printed. In the preface to his next play, *The Double Dealer*, he writes :—" I grant that for a man to talk to himself appears absurd and unnatural, and indeed it is so in most cases; but the circumstances which may attend the occasion make great alteration. It oftentimes happens to a man to have designs which require him to himself [*sic*] and in their nature cannot admit of a confidant. Such for certain is all villainy, and other less mischievous intentions may be very improper to be communicated to a second person. In such a case, therefore, the audience must observe whether the person upon the stage takes any notice of them at all or no. For if he supposes anyone to be by when he talks to himself, it is monstrous and ridiculous to the last degree. Nay, not only in this case, but in any part of a play, if there is expressed any knowledge of an audience, it is insufferable. But otherwise, when a man in soliloquy reasons with himself, and *pro's* and *con's*, and weighs all his designs, we ought not to imagine that this man either talks to us or to himself; he is only thinking, and thinking such matters as were inexcusable folly in him to speak. But because we are concealed spectators of the plot in agitation, and the poet finds it necessary to let us know the whole mystery of his contrivance, he is willing to inform us of this person's thoughts; and to that end is forced to make use of the expedient of speech, no other better way being yet invented for the communication of thought."

In *The Double Dealer*, written some two years after *The Old Bachelor*, Congreve is still in the imitative stage. In this play the general design is modeled upon that of Molière's *Tartuffe*, and, like that work, its artistic unity is injured by the violent introduction of an illogical element, forced in to save what was intended to be a comedy from turning out a tragedy. For the logical outcome of the *Tartuffe* is truly tragical, not comical. Orgon's infatuation with Tartuffe, his incapacity for seeing through the character of the impostor, his folly in putting himself so thoroughly into the power of that impostor,—all this should consistently result in the ruin of the good man, in the triumph of the bad. Nothing could prevent this but the forced and inartistic introduction of the King's officer with his sycophantic praise of his monarch's great discernment and lofty soul. Similarly in *The Double Dealer*, the folly of Lord Touchwood and of Mellefonte in trusting Maskwell in spite of plain proofs of his insincerity, should have logically resulted in the triumph of villainy. This result is avoided only by making the villain leave unguarded so wide a gap in the fence of his deceit that not even so trusting a fool as Mellefonte could help noticing it. This serious defect was so apparent at the early representations, that the play was practically a failure in spite of its brilliant wit and the genuine comedy of some of its scenes.

Coming now to detailed resemblances between *The Double Dealer* and works of Molière, we notice that the character of Lady Froth, the best comedy character in the play, described by Congreve in his play-bill as "a great coquette, pretender to poetry, wit and learning,"—this delightful bluestocking who babbles of "Racine and Dacier upon Aristotle," is a compound of the two sisters in *Les Précieuses Ridicules*,—Cathos, who considered extempore verses . . . "the very touchstone of genius," and Madelon, whose special talent consisted in turning the whole Roman history into madrigals. Scene 10 of Act I. of *Les Précieuses Ridicules*, where Mascarille reads his verses to the ladies, and the second scene of Act I. of *Le Misanthrope*, where Oronte demands that Alceste should criticise his sonnet,—these are the prototypes of the tenth scene of Act III. of *The Double Dealer*, where Lady Froth receives the admiration of Mr. Brisk for her poem of "The Coachman in the Dairy." I give this episode entire, as it is in Congreve's best style and may challenge comparison with the original.

Lady Froth. Then you think that episode between Susan, the dairymaid, and our coachman is not amiss; you know I may suppose the dairy in town as well as in the country.

Brisk. Incomparable, let me perish! But then, being an heroic poem, had not you better call him a charioteer? Charioteer sounds great; besides, your ladyship's coachman having a red face, and you comparing him to the sun; and you know the sun is called Heaven's charioteer.

Lady F. Oh, infinitely better! I am extremely beholden to you for the hint; stay, we'll read over those half a score lines again. [Pulls out a paper.] Let me see here, you know what goes before,—the comparison, you know. [Reads]

 For as the sun shines every day
 So of our coachman I may say——

B. I'm afraid that simile won't do in wet weather; because you say the sun shines every day.

Lady F. No, for the sun it won't, but it will do for the coachman: for you know there's most occasion for a coach in wet weather.

B. Right, right, that saves all.

Lady F. Then, I don't say the sun shines all the day, but that he peeps now and then; yet he does shine all the day too, you know, though we don't see him.

B. Right; but the vulgar will never comprehend that.

Lady F. Well, you shall hear. Let me see. [Reads]

 For as the sun shines every day,
 So, of our coachman I may say,
 He shows his drunken, fiery face,
 Just as the sun does, more or less.

B. That's right, all's well, all's well!—"more or less."

Lady F. [Reads]

 And when at night his labour's done,
 Then, too, like Heaven's charioteer the sun—

Ay, charioteer does better.

 Into the dairy he descends,
 And there his whipping and his driving ends;
 There he's secure from danger of a bilk,
 His fare is paid him, and he sets in milk.

For Susan, you know, is Thetis, and so——

B. Incomparably well and proper, egad! But I have one exception to make: don't you think bilk—(I know it's good rhyme)—but don't you think "bilk" and "fare" too like a hackney coachman?

Lady F. I swear and vow, I am afraid so. And yet our Jehu was a hackney coachman when my lord took him.

B. Was he? I'm answered if Jehu was a hackney coachman. You may put that in the marginal notes though, to prevent criticism. Only mark it with a small asterism, and say, "Jehu was formerly a hackney coach man."

Lady F. I will; you'd oblige me extremely to write notes to the whole poem.

B. With all my heart and soul, and proud of the vast honor, let me perish!

The same scene contains a fire of scandal-mongering epigrams lighted by the torches which wave so merrily in the hands of Célimène, Clitandre and Acaste as they march through the 5th scene of the 2nd Act of *Le Misanthrope*. It may be worth while to notice in passing that the concluding couplet of the 3rd Act of *The Double Dealer* is nothing but a rimed expression of the thought contained in Swift's famous definition of happiness,—

"the perpetual possession of being well deceived."

The Double Dealer is the last of Congreve's plays that shows strong detailed resemblances to specific works of Molière. In this play Congreve is still in the imitative stage : his characters, though witty, are seldom other than conventional and are often not clearly distinguished. Sir Paul Pliant and Lord Froth are practically one and the same : Mr. Brisk and Mr. Careless could speak each other's speeches with entire dramatic propriety : Cynthia and Mellefonte are excellent young people, but hardly anything more. The pernicious habit of long soliloquies, imitated from Molière and noticeable in *The Old Bachelor*, is carried to even greater lengths in *The Double Dealer*. But when we remember that when Congreve wrote this play he was only 23, our wonder is not that the defects are so many, but that they are so few.

Though of far more intrinsic interest, Congreve's third and fifth plays, *Love for Love* and *The Way of the World*, cannot long detain us here : their very originality excludes all but a small portion of them from the field marked off by the limitations of our subject. In characters they owe nothing to Molière save the types of gossipy, malicious fine ladies and gentlemen,—Mrs. Frail, Scandal and Tattle, in *Love for Love;* Witwoud and Millamant, in *The Way of the World.* In general structure we still see the influence of Molière's style: the action is completed within a few hours: the scenes, ordinary and realistic interiors such as a drawing-room or a coffee-house, are seldom changed. Turning from resemblances to contrasts, we notice that in the principal characters of these two great plays, Congreve is as thoroughly English as Molière is French. Foresight, Sir Sampson Legend, Ben Legend, Sir Wilfull Witwoud, Lady Wishfort, are all of true British grain; while the teasing perplexities of the Congreve plots carry us far from that simplicity of construction characteristic of Molière. In ethical tone and in artistic diction, Congreve, it must be confessed, suffers by comparison with Molière. This is due, partly, to the lighter and more superficial nature of the Englishman, partly to the bad English models which set the fashion for him, and partly to his youth when he wrote.

Congreve's last and greatest play was written when he was but thirty. At that age Molière had written nothing but a few farces imitated from the Italian. All the deep experiences of life recorded in his great comedies were yet to come to him: when they came they fell upon a mind tried in the school of adversity, thoughtful, mature, refined. Many like experiences *may* have come to Congreve in the 28 years that followed his masterpiece and in which he wrote almost nothing; if they did come, they fell upon barren soil: unwatered by the dew of emotion, they withered and died. Yet in some obscure corner of Congreve's hard and cynical heart there must have been one soft and tender spot, for into the mouth of a Mrs. Marwood he has put one divine phrase: "Say what you will, 'tis better to be left than never to have been loved."—a sentiment which, hardly better expressed, reappears in Tennyson's famous,

"'Tis better to have loved and lost,
Than never to have loved at all."

This brief study of Congreve may fitly close with a judgment upon him delivered by a celebrated Frenchman,—no less a man than Voltaire. In his *Lettres sur les Anglais* he writes: "Mr. Congreve raised the glory of comedy to a greater height than any English writer before or since his time. He wrote only a few plays, but they are excellent in their kind. The laws of the drama are strictly observed in them. They abound with characters, all which are shadowed with the utmost delicacy, and we do not meet with so much as one low or coarse jest. (!) The language is everywhere that of men of fashion, but their actions are those of knaves, a proof that he was perfectly well acquainted with human nature and frequented what we call polite company."

From *The Way of the World* in 1700 to *The School for Scandal* in 1777 is a long step, yet this distance must be traveled before we can meet an English comedy writer with wit enough to erect upon the foundations of Molière a superstructure after the fashion of Congreve. During this long period, while there had arisen no great writer to carry on the Congreve tradition, the art of play-writing (of putting together what the French call the " well-made piece ")—this had been practised by a succession of clever men, Vanbrugh, Farquhar, Cibber, Gay, Hoadley, Coleman, Garrick, and had resulted in a decided improvement in what may be called the mechanics of construction. The advantage which Sheridan thus inherited has been described by Taine ("History of English Literature," Book III., Chap. I., Section 10): "The farce-writer of to-day sees that the catastrophe of half of Molière's plays is ridiculous; nay, many of them can produce effects better than Molière; in the long run they succeed in stripping the theatre of all awkwardness and circumlocution. A piquant style, and perfect machinery; pungency in all the words and animation in all the scenes; a superabundance of wit and marvels of ingenuity; over all this, a true physical activity and the secret pleasure of depicting and justifying oneself, of public self-glorification: here is the foundation of the *School for Scandal*, here the source of the talent and the success of Sheridan."

Many sources have been suggested whence Sheridan may have drawn his *School for Scandal*, yet after all has been said it is difficult to believe that he is much indebted to any authors save Molière and the Restoration comedy writers who copied him. The first indication of this is in the title of the play, modeled upon the *School for Wives* and the *School for Husbands* of Molière. This conception of the scandalous college (after *Le Misanthrope*) seems to have been the nucleus of the play, and the manuscript draft of the scandal-mongering conversation shows a brutal coarseness of wit, suggesting a close study of Wycherley and Farquhar. Through repeated revisions this coarseness was gradually polished away until it resulted in the present version: even this is somewhat broader than 19th century ears are accustomed to, and suffers by comparison with the tone of good taste preserved in the corresponding scenes of *Le Misanthrope*. This will be illustrated by an extract further on: let it suffice now to recall attention to the title of the play and to the prominence assigned to Lady Sneerwell and Mrs. Candor in the opening scene as indications of the probability that Sheridan's original intention was to write a comedy satirizing those fashionable lovers of scandal whom he had often listened to at Bath and whose prototypes he found already done to the life in Molière and in Congreve. But this he must have found too thin a thread upon which to hang a five-act play, and he accordingly twisted in with it another strand,—the story of the Teazles and of the two brothers Surface. The character of Sir Peter Teazle, originally intended to be merely a vulgar city merchant, was gradually sublimated and assimilated to that of his prototype Alceste in *Le Misanthrope:* when the outline is completed we find him placed outside the envenomed circle of gossips, as was Alceste, and voicing, as did he, the comment and the rebuke of the just-minded spectator. Sir Peter has the violence of Sir Sampson Legend without his vindictiveness; he has all the honesty of Alceste without his moroseness. In the character and actions of Joseph Surface, Sheridan has again drawn heavily upon Molière,—this time upon Tartuffe. Both Joseph and Tartuffe rise by hypocrisy; the object at which they aim is the same, and whoever will compare the arguments addressed by Tartuffe to

Elmire (*Tartuffe*, IV., 5), with those addressed by Joseph Surface to Lady Teazle (*School for Scandal*, IV., 3), will see that Sheridan's treatment of this delicate situation is directly based upon Molière's. In the management of his *dénouement*, in the working up of the wonderfully effective climax wherein the hypocrite is unmasked, Sheridan, it seems to me, has surpassed not only Molière, who is here confessedly weak, but also Congreve, who, in the 5th Act of the *Double Dealer*, evidently saw that a strong situation was here demanded, but was as evidently unable to bring it about.

In conclusion, I shall present the treatment of the same theme by each of the authors under consideration. This theme shall be that which gives its title to Sheridan's play,—the representation of that careless, easy, malicious conversation which serves as the small change of fashionable society. In Molière the scene selected is the 5th of the 2nd Act of *Le Misanthrope:* the principal characters are Célimène, the fine lady; Alceste, her honest and plain-speaking lover; Acaste and Clitandre, Marquises.

Clit. Egad! madam, I have just come from the Louvre, where Cléonte, at the levee, made himself supremely ridiculous. Has he no friend who could give him some charitable advice on his behaviour?

Céli. It is true that he sadly compromises his reputation; his manners everywhere at once strike us as odd; and when after a short absence we see him again, he seems even more absurd than before.

Aca. 'Gad! talking of absurd people, I have just had to bear with that most trying of tedious bores, the arguer Damon; if you will believe me, he kept me out of my sedan-chair in the broiling sun for a whole hour.

Céli. He certainly is a strange talker, and knows how to make long speeches with no meaning in them. No one understands a word of what he says; and in all that we hear, there is nothing but noise.

Eli. (to *Philinte*). This is no bad beginning, and the conversation is in a fair way against our neighbors.

Clit. Timante, madam, is another original.

Céli. He is a man all mystery from head to foot. In passing he casts upon one a bewildered glance, and with nothing to do is always busy. Grimaces abound in whatever he says, and he wearies one to death with his ceremonies. In the midst of a general conversation he has always some secret to whisper, and that secret turns out to be nothing. He makes a wonder of the merest trifle, and even wishes you "Good morning" mysteriously in your ear.

Aca. And Gérald, madam?

Céli. Oh! the tedious boaster! You never see him come down from his noble pedestal. He is always mixing in the best society, and never quotes anyone less than duke, prince, or princess. Rank has turned his head, and all his talk is of horses, carriages and dogs. He "thou's" people of the highest position, and the word "sir" is with him quite obsolete.

Clit. It is said that he is on the best terms with Bélise.

Céli. Ah! the poor creature; and what dull company she is! I suffer martyrdom when she comes to see me. In vain do I tax my powers to the utmost, to find out what to say to her; the barrenness of her talk destroys every attempt at conversation. It is useless to have recourse to the most commonplace topics to overcome her stupid silence; the fine weather, the rain, the cold, and the heat are soon exhausted. Yet her visits, in themselves so unwelcome, drag their weary length along, and you may consult the clock and yawn twenty times, but she stirs no more than a log of wood.

Aca. And what do you think of Adraste?

Céli. Ah! what intolerable pride! He is a man puffed up with conceit, always dissatisfied with the Court, and making it his business daily to inveigh against it. There is neither office, place nor living given away without some injustice having been done to the important personage he fancies himself to be.

Clit. But young Cléon, who is visited by the best society, what do you say of him?

Céli. That his cook has all the merit, and that it is to his table that each one pays respect.

Eli. He takes care to provide the most dainty dishes.

Céli. Yes, but I wish he would not provide himself; and I consider his stupid person a most unpleasant dish, which, to my mind, spoils the taste of all the others.

Phil. His uncle, Damis, is greatly esteemed: what do you say of him, madam?

Céli. He is one of my friends.

Phil. He is a gentleman, and has plenty of good sense.

Céli. Yes; only the display of cleverness he makes vexes me beyond measure. He is always stiff and formal, and in all he says you can feel the effort he is making to utter some witticism. Since he has taken it into his head to think himself clever, he is so exacting that nothing can please his taste. He tries to see defects in all that is written; thinks that to bestow praise is not worthy of a man of intelligence; that it is a sign of knowledge to find fault with everything, the part of fools to admire and to laugh; and that in never approving the writings of our time he shows his superiority to other people. He even finds fault with ordinary conversations, and will not condescend to utter common things; but, his arms crossed on his breast, looks down with contempt from the height of his intellect on all that is said.

Aca. Demmit, madam, his very picture!

Clit. Your skill in drawing character is admirable, madam.

Alc. Go on, go on, my dear courtly friends; no one is spared, and each will have his turn; yet, let any one of those people now appear, and we shall see you rush in haste to meet him, offer your hand, and with a flattering embrace protest you are his sincere friend.

Clit. Why do you call us to account? If you object to what is said, you had better address your reproaches to this lady.

Alc. No, upon my soul, no! It is you who deserve the blame; your fawning smiles draw from her these slanderous descriptions; her satirical turn of mind is constantly encouraged by the criminal incense of your flattery. She would find raillery less to her taste if she knew that it is not approved of. Thus it is that flatterers are always responsible for the vices spread among mankind.

Phil. But why show such deep interest for those people? You would be the first to condemn in them the defects we find fault with.

Céli. But must not our friend always show opposition? You surely would not have him think like everybody else, and must he not display everywhere the spirit of contradiction with which Heaven has blessed him? What others think never satisfies him; he is always of the opposite opinion, and he would fear to pass for a vulgar-minded man if he were observed to agree with anyone. The privilege of contradicting has such charms for him, that he is often in arms against himself; and to hear his own thoughts expressed by others is sufficient to make him oppose them.

Here we notice that the method of presentation is very simple and not particularly dramatic; while it is true that the interest is centred on the heroine by giving her all the long character sketches to declaim, there is no clash of mind against mind, no repartee, no conflict of character with character until Alceste breaks in near the close of the scene.

Congreve's method is very different in detail, as witness the following from the 2nd scene of the 2nd Act of *The Way of the World*. Here the principal characters are Millamant, the fine lady; Mirabell, her lover, who grudges her society to everyone but himself; Witwoud, the would-be wit.

[Enter *Mrs. Millamant, Witwoud* and *Mincing*.]

Mir. Here she comes, i' faith, full sail, with her fan spread and her streamers out, and a shoal of fools for tenders; ha, no, I cry her mercy!

Mrs. Fain. I see but one poor empty sculler, and he tows her woman after him.

Mir. (to *Mrs. Millamant*). You seem to be unattended, madam—you used to have the *beau monde* throng after you; and a flock of gay fine perukes hovering round you.

Wit. Like moths about a candle. I had like to have lost my comparison for want of breath.

Mrs. Mil. O, I have denied myself airs to-day; I have walked as fast through the crowd—

Wit. As a favourite just disgraced, and with as few followers.

Mrs. Mil. Dear Mr. Witwoud, truce with your similitudes; for I'm as sick of 'em——

Wit. As a physician of a good air. I cannot help it, madam, though 'tis against myself.

Mrs. Mil. Yet again! Mincing, stand between me and his wit.

Wit. Do, Mrs. Mincing, like a screen before a great fire. I confess I do blaze to-day,—I am too bright.

Mrs. Fain. But, dear Millamant, why were you so long?

Mrs. Mil. Long! Lord, have I not made violent haste? I have asked every living thing I met for you; I have inquired after you, as after a new fashion.

Wit. Madam, truce with your similitudes. No, you met her husband, and did not ask him for her.

Mrs. Mil. By your leave, Witwoud, that were like inquiring after an old fashion, to ask a husband for his wife.

Wit. Hum, a hit! a hit, a palpable hit! I confess it.

Mrs. Fain. You were dressed before I came abroad.

Mrs. Mil. Ay, that's true. O, but then I had —Mincing, what had I? Why was I so long?

Min. O, mem, your la'ship stayed to peruse a packet of letters.

Mrs. Mil. O ay, letters—I had letters—I am persecuted with letters—I hate letters—nobody knows how to write letters, and yet one has 'em, one does not know why. They serve one to pin up one's hair.

Wit. Is that the way? Pray, madam, do you pin up your hair with all your letters? I find I must keep copies.

Mrs. Mil. Only with those in verse, Mr. Witwoud. I never pin up my hair with prose. I think I tried once, Mincing.

Min. O, mem, I shall never forget it.

Mrs. Mil. Ay, poor Mincing tift and tift all the morning.

Min. Till I had the cramp in my fingers, I'll vow, mem: and all to no purpose. But when your la'ship pins it up with poetry, it sits so pleasant the next day as anything, and is so pure and so crips.

Wit. Indeed, so crips?

Min. You're such a critic, Mr. Witwoud.

Mrs. Mil. Mirabell, did you take exceptions last night? O, ay, and went away. Now I think on't, I'm angry—no, now I think on't, I'm pleased, for I believe I gave you some pain.

Mir. Does that please you?

Mrs. Mil. Infinitely; I love to give pain.

Mir. You would affect a cruelty which is not in your nature; your true vanity is in the power of pleasing.

Mrs. Mil. Oh, I ask you pardon for that. One's cruelty is one's power; and when one parts with one's cruelty, one parts with one's power; and when one has parted with that, I fancy one's old and ugly.

Mir. Ay, ay, suffer your cruelty to ruin the object of your power, to destroy your lover,— and then how vain, how lost a thing you'll be! Nay, 'tis true: you are no longer handsome when you've lost your lover; your beauty dies upon the instant; for beauty is the lover's gift; 'tis he bestows your charms—your glass is all a cheat. The ugly and the old, whom the looking-glass mortifies, yet after commendation can be flattered by it, and discover beauties in it; for that reflects our praises, rather than your face.

Mrs. Mil. O, the vanity of these men! Fainall, d'ye hear him? If they did not commend us, we were not handsome! Now you must know they could not commend one if one was not handsome. Beauty the lover's gift! Lord, what is a lover, that it can give? Why, one makes lovers as fast as one pleases, and they live as long as one pleases, and they die as soon as one pleases; and then, if one pleases, one makes more.

Wit. Very pretty. Why, you make no more of making of lovers, madam, than of making so many card-matches.

Mrs. Mil. One no more owes one's beauty to a lover, than one's wit to an echo. They can but reflect what we look and say; vain, empty things if we are silent or unseen, and want a being.

Mir. Yet to those two vain, empty things you owe the two greatest pleasures of your life.
Mrs. Mil. How so?
Mir. To your lover you owe the pleasure of hearing yourselves praised; and to an echo the pleasure of hearing yourselves talk.
Wit. But I know a lady that loves talking so incessantly, she won't give an echo fair play; she has that everlasting rotation of tongue, that an echo must wait till she dies before it can catch her last words.

In this presentation the heroine is not only witty herself, but is also the cause of wit in others. Epigrams, repartee and similes follow each other fast and brilliant as shower of stars from exploding rocket. There is nothing serious, as in the tempersome speeches of Molière's hero; all is lightness, gaiety, ease. The *bon mots* are distributed among the various characters with an evenness that amounts almost to balance.

From Sheridan we take a part of the 2nd scene of the 2nd Act of the *School for Scandal:* the college of gossips is holding a session in Lady Sneerwell's house, with that lady as the presiding genius.

Mrs. Can. Now, I'll die; but you are so scandalous, I'll forswear your society.

Lady Teaz. What's the matter, Mrs. Candour?

Mrs. Can. They'll not allow our friend Miss Vermilion to be handsome.

Lady Sneer. Oh, surely she is a pretty woman.

Crab. I am very glad you think so, ma'am.

Mrs. Can. She has a charming fresh colour.

Lady Teaz. Yes, when it is fresh put on.

Mrs. Can. Oh, fie! I'll swear her colour is natural: I have seen it come and go!

Lady Teaz. I dare swear you have, ma'am: it goes off at night, and comes again in the morning.

Sir Ben. True, ma'am, it not only comes and goes; but what's more, egad, her maid can fetch and carry it!

Mrs. Can. Ha! ha! ha! how I hate to hear you talk so! But surely, now, her sister is, or was, very handsome.

Crab. Who? Mrs. Evergreen? O Lord! she's six-and-fifty if she's an hour!

Mrs. Can. Now positively you wrong her; fifty-two or fifty-three is the utmost—and I don't think she looks more.

Sir Ben. Ah! there's no judging by her looks, unless one could see her face.

Lady Sneer. Well, well, if Mrs. Evergreen does not take some pains to repair the ravages of time, you must allow she effects it with great ingenuity; and surely that's better than the careless manner in which the widow Ochre caulks her wrinkles.

Sir Ben. Nay, now, Lady Sneerwell, you are severe upon the widow. Come, come, 'tis not that she paints so ill—but, when she has finished her face, she joins it on so badly to her neck, that she looks like a mended statue, in which the connoisseur may see at once that the head is modern, though the trunk's antique.

Crab. Ha! ha! ha! Well said, nephew!

Mrs. Can. Ha! ha! ha! Well, you make me laugh; but I vow I hate you for it. What do you think of Miss Simper?

Sir Ben. Why, she has very pretty teeth.

Lady Teaz. Yes, and on that account, when she is neither speaking nor laughing (which very seldom happens), she never absolutely shuts her mouth, but leaves it always on ajar, as it were—thus. [*Shows her teeth.*

Mrs. Can. How can you be so ill-natured?

Lady Teaz. Nay, I allow even that's better than the pains Mrs. Prim takes to conceal her losses in front. She draws her mouth till it positively resembles the aperture of a poor's-box, and all her words appear to slide out edgewise as it were—thus: *How do you do, madam? Yes, madam.* [*Mimics.*

Lady Sneer. Very well, Lady Teazle; I see you can be a little severe.

Lady Teaz. In defence of a friend, it is but justice. But here comes Sir Peter to spoil our pleasantry.

Enter SIR PETER TEAZLE.

Sir Pet. Ladies, your most obedient.—[*Aside.*] Mercy on me, here is the whole set! a character dead at every word, I suppose.

Mrs. Can. I am rejoiced you are come, Sir

Peter. They have been so censorious—and Lady Teazle as bad as any one.

Sir Pet. That must be very distressing to you, indeed, Mrs. Candour.

Mrs Can. Oh, they will allow good qualities to nobody; not even good nature to our friend Mrs. Pursy.

Lady Teaz. What, the fat dowager who was at Mrs. Quadrille's last night?

Mrs. Can. Nay, her bulk is her misfortune; and, when she takes so much pains to get rid of it, you ought not to reflect on her.

Lady Sneer. That's very true, indeed.

Lady Teaz. Yes, I know she almost lives on acids and small whey; laces herself by pulleys; and often, in the hottest noon in summer, you may see her on a little squat pony, with her hair plaited up behind like a drummer's, and puffing round the Ring on a full trot.

Mrs. Can. I thank you, Lady Teazle, for defending her.

Sir Pet. Yes, a good defence truly.

Mrs. Can. Truly, Lady Teazle is as censorious as Miss Sallow.

Crab. Yes, and she is a curious being to pretend to be censorious—an awkward gawky, without any one good point under heaven.

Mrs. Can. Positively you shall not be so very severe. Miss Sallow is a near relation of mine by marriage, and as for her person, great allowance is to be made; for, let me tell you, a woman labours under many disadvantages who tries to pass for a girl of six-and-thirty.

Lady Sneer. Though, surely, she is handsome still—and for the weakness in her eyes, considering how much she reads by candlelight, it is not to be wondered at.

Mrs. Can. True, and then as to her manner; upon my word I think it is particularly graceful, considering she never had the least education; for you know her mother was a Welsh milliner, and her father a sugar-baker at Bristol.

Sir Ben. Ah! you are both of you too good-natured!

Sir Pet. Yes, damned good-natured! This, their own relation! mercy on me! [*Aside.*

Mrs. Can. For my part, I own I cannot bear to hear a friend ill spoken of.

Sir Pet. No, to be sure!

Sir Ben. Oh! you are of a moral turn. Mrs. Candour and I can sit for an hour and hear Lady Stucco talk sentiment.

Lady Teaz. Nay, I vow Lady Stucco is very well with the dessert after dinner; for she's just like the French fruit one cracks for mottoes—made up of paint and proverb.

Mrs. Can. Well, I will never join in ridiculing a friend; and so I constantly tell my cousin Ogle, and you all know what pretensions she has to be critical on beauty.

Crab. Oh, to be sure! she has herself the oddest countenance that ever was seen; 'tis a collection of features from all the different countries of the globe.

Sir Ben. So she has, indeed—an Irish front——

Crab. Caledonian locks——

Sir Ben. Dutch nose——

Crab. Austrian lips——
Sir Ben. Complexion of a Spaniard——
Crab. And teeth à *la Chinoise*——
Sir Ben. In short, her face resembles a *table d'hôte* at Spa—where no two guests are of a nation——
Crab. Or a congress at the close of a general war—wherein all the members, even to her eyes, appear to have a different interest, and her nose and chin are the only parties likely to join issue.
Mrs. Can. Ha! ha! ha!
Sir Pet. Mercy on my life!—a person they dine with twice a week! [*Aside.*
Mrs. Can. Nay, but I vow you shall not carry the laugh off so—for give me leave to say that Mrs. Ogle——
Sir Pet. Madam, madam, I beg your pardon—there's no stopping these good gentlemen's tongues. But when I tell you, Mrs. Candour, that the lady they are abusing is a particular friend of mine, I hope you'll not take her part.
Lady Sneer. Ha! ha! ha! well said, Sir Peter! but you are a cruel creature—too phlegmatic yourself for a jest, and too peevish to allow wit in others.
Sir Pet. Ah, madam, true wit is more nearly allied to good nature than your ladyship is aware of.
Lady Teaz. True, Sir Peter; I believe they are so near akin that they can never be united.
Sir Ben. Or, rather, suppose them man and wife, because one seldom sees them together.
Lady Teaz. But Sir Peter is such an enemy

to scandal, I believe he would have it put down by parliament.

Sir Pet. 'Fore heaven, madam, if they were to consider the sporting with reputation of as much importance as poaching on manors, and pass an act for the preservation of fame as well as game, I believe many would thank them for the bill.

Lady Sneer. O Lud! Sir Peter; would you deprive us of our privileges?

Sir Pet. Ay, madam; and then no person should be permitted to kill characters and run down reputations but qualified old maids and disappointed widows.

Lady Sneer. Go, you monster!

Mrs. Can. But, surely, you would not be quite so severe on those who only report what they hear?

Sir Pet. Yes, madam, I would have law merchant for them too; and in all cases of slander currency, whenever the drawer of the lie was not to be found, the injured parties should have a right to come on any of the indorsers.

Crab. Well, for my part, I believe there never was a scandalous tale without some foundation.

In this treatment we see a combination of Molière's method with Congreve's: Sir Peter's attitude is similar to that of Alceste, although we notice he is less skilfully connected by the dramatist with the main action: two of his most important speeches are given as *asides*. In the balancing distribution of his good lines to several characters instead of centering them upon one, Sheridan has followed Congreve. The wit of the latter, it seems to me, is superior to that of the former, for Congreve detects and points out real resemblances between things apparently incongruous, while Sheridan throws a garish light upon resemblances that are often merely whimsical and fantastical. Congreve presents us with a miniature of life firm in its drawing, rich in its coloring; Sheridan gives us a caricature, wonderfully clever in its depiction of salient features, but still a caricature. For the purpose of interesting and amusing an average audience, the Sheridan method is undoubtedly the more effective: given the conditions of the drama to-day, it is therefore theatrically the better. Yet, when a majority of us shall have risen from what Mill justly calls our present low plane of culture, we shall realize, I think, that despite the defects of his age Congreve is a greater artist than Sheridan, and that greater than either is Molière.

II.

IS THE ACTOR'S ART UNWORTHY?

Few things are more humorous than the sight of a humorist taking himself seriously. Such an edifying spectacle is presented to the world in the person of Mr. Augustine Birrell, barrister-at-law, author of "Obiter Dicta" and other delightful brochures. Readers of these essays will agree with me, I am sure, that humor is Mr. Birrell's strong point, and that so long as he sticks to his last hardly a shoemaker of their acquaintance could do better. But in his "Essay on Actors" Mr. Birrell has not only made the mistake intimated above, but has also committed the literary crime of printing his opinions upon a subject with which he seems to be but superficially acquainted. His condemnation of the actor's art as unworthy is a conclusion which he reaches by a method of argument anything but judicial—a method which is, in fact, nothing more nor less than a special plea for the prosecution. Such a treatment of a literary topic doubtless came naturally to him as a result of his training as a lawyer, whose business it must often be to make out a strong case by the simple process of selecting from a mass of testimony all the facts that tell for his side and suppressing or belittling all those which tell for the other side. This is good forensics; it is excellent practice for debaters; but it is not criticism.

The actor's art, says Mr. Birrell, is unworthy of an artist, and the first argument he brings forward in proof of this general proposition is the argument from antiquity. By a trite story he proves, easily enough, that among the Romans the actor's art was held in light esteem; there he rests this portion of his case, leaving the impression upon the reader's mind that the wise men of the ancient world thought as little of the histrio as does Mr. Birrell.

To this argument there are two replies. In the first place, the argument from antiquity has here little force, because the conditions of ancient and modern life are so vastly different. Life in modern society is far deeper, richer, fuller and more complex than in ancient society; the art of the modern actor, whose business it is to represent this life, is therefore deeper, richer, fuller and more complex than that of his ancient prototype. It calls for a higher intellectuality, and may reasonably be thought as much superior to ancient acting as modern literature is to ancient. The condemnation of the actor's art, then, by the Roman world was a condemnation of a very simple thing with which that world was well acquainted. To apply this condemnation to another and a very complex thing, of which that world knew nothing, is absurd and illogical.

In the second place, if the opinion of antiquity upon a fine art is to be quoted, why quote only the opinion of the Romans, one of the most inartistic peoples that has ever existed and one that is conspicuous for its failure in the particular art under discussion? In war and in law the Romans were great and original; in the fine arts they were weak and imitators of the Greeks. Roman painting, so far as we know anything about it, is based upon Greek masters; Roman sculpture is the same; Roman architecture fails to unite the beautiful with the useful. In Epic poetry Virgil is confessedly the imitator of Homer; in Lyric, Horace is, strictly speaking, not a poet at all, but an extremely clever man of the world, expressing his sententious maxims in art forms which he learned from the Greek lyrists; in dramatic poetry the comedy writers, Plautus and Terence, are little more than adapters of the Greek writers Menander and Apollodorus, while in tragedy Rome cannot show a single name more distinguished than that of the turgid Seneca. The opinion of such a people upon a question of fine art is worth very little; the opinion of their masters, the Greeks, may be worth a great deal. Now, among the Greeks the actor's art was not held in light esteem. It was a common custom for the poet who was honored by receiving from the State a prize for his play, himself to enact the principal part in that play. This was done not only by Aeschylus, but also by the most artistic poet of the ancient world,—Sophocles,

* * * whose even-balanced soul
From first youth tested up to extreme old age,

Business could not make dull, nor passion wild;
Who saw life steadily and saw it whole;
The mellow glory of the Attic stage,
Singer of sweet Colonus and his child.

Turning from ancient to modern times, Mr. Birrell next attempts to show the actor's art unworthy because from its very nature it leaves little or no record to account for his fame. This argument proves too much: it applies equally well to great singers like Jenny Lind and Patti; yet who shall call their art unworthy? It applies also to such painters as Zeuxis and Apelles, of whose work there remains nothing but the names; extend your time-limit but a very little and it will apply also to such painters as Tintoretto and Reubens, whose handiwork is fast fading from the perishable canvas; yet is their art unworthy?

In support of this portion of his argument Mr. Birrell commits himself to the astounding declaration that "This, perhaps, is why no man of lofty genius or character has ever condescended to remain an actor." (!) Now this remark betrays such a profound ignorance of the history of the drama as to make one believe that Mr. Birrell has never heard of a country called France and of a certain actor-poet, there somewhat esteemed, called Molière. As to character, Molière was one of the most beautiful and unselfish souls the world has ever seen. His life was one long struggle against folly and superstition. His death was hastened by his untiring devotion to the members of the little company who depended upon him for support. As to his genius, I will merely quote from the words of an English critic not given to overpraise of anything French. In his essay on "The French Play in London," Matthew Arnold writes: "*The Misanthrope* and *The Tartuffe* are comedy, but they are comedy in verse, poetic comedy. * * * Immense power has gone to the making of them,—a world of vigorous sense, piercing observation, pathetic mediation, profound criticism of life. Molière had also one great advantage as a dramatist over Shakespeare: he wrote for a more developed theatre, a more developed society. Moreover, he was at the same time, probably, by nature a better theatre-poet than Shakespeare; he had a keener sense for theatrical situation. Shakespeare is not rightly to be called, as Goethe calls him, an epitomator rather than a dramatist; but he may rightly be called rather a dramatist than a theatre-poet. Molière—and here his French nature stood him in good stead—was a theatre-poet of the very first order." Now this man was an actor during his whole life; yet Mr. Birrell would have us believe that "no man of lofty genius or character has ever condescended to remain an actor."

Other instances, such as that of Edwin Booth, might be detailed to overthrow Mr. Birrell's absurd generalization, but for the purposes of the argument the case of Molière will perhaps suffice.

Mr. Birrell then quotes from the "Sonnets of Shakespeare" and the "Memoirs of Macready" and of Mrs. Siddons to show that these actors despised their calling, and concludes with another generalization that must make logicians weep: "The volunteered testimony of actors," he says, "is both large in bulk and valuable in quality, and it is all on my side."

To dispose of the generalization first, there is plenty of testimony to show that fine actors do not despise their calling.

It is too much, perhaps, to expect that Mr. Birrell should be acquainted with books published in a place so far beyond his horizon-line as New York, yet if he could stretch his intellectual vision that far he would discover there in the "Autobiography of Joseph Jefferson" and in Winter's "Life of Edwin Booth" considerable testimony that is not on his side Some acquaintance with the utterances of the leading actor of his own country Mr. Birrell might reasonably be supposed to possess. Yet he seems never to have heard of the following words of Sir Henry Irving, spoken nearly seven years ago before the Philosophical Institution of Edinburgh : " * * *   every actor who is more than a mere machine, and who has an ideal of any kind, has a duty which lies beyond the scope of his personal ambition. His art must be something to hold in reverence if he wishes others to hold it in esteem. There is nothing of chance about this work. All, actors and audience alike, must bear in mind that the whole scheme of the higher drama is not to be regarded as a game in life which can be played with varying success. Its present intention may be to interest and amuse, but its deeper purpose is earnest, intense, sincere." These are hardly the words of a man who despises his calling.

As to Shakespeare's testimony, to quote the passing emotion expressed in the one hundred and tenth sonnet as if it were his settled conviction as to the unworthiness of his calling, this is as absurd as to say that he deliberately attempted suicide because, in the sixty-sixth sonnet, he wrote,

> Tired with all these, for restful death I cry,

absurd as it would be to represent Shakespeare as a weak-minded railer at destiny because in the twenty-ninth sonnet he tells us that he beweeps his outcast state, troubles deaf heaven with bootless cries and curses his fate. All such outbursts are lyrical—that is, they are the powerful expression of some single and transient emotion. From any single utterance, little or nothing can be inferred as to the writer's permanent convictions on any large topic.

Finally, Mr. Birrell gives away his whole case in the last paragraph but one of his essay. He there allows that the actor's calling is "lawful, useful, delightful," but still he will not allow that it is "worthy." But one of the three concessions here granted is necessary, since things useful are things worthy. The actor's art is useful because, like that of the poet, the painter, the sculptor, it tends to increase the amount of pleasurable emotions and so tends to make life richer and fuller. Well has it been said by one, himself an actor: "If he (the actor) can smite water from the rock of one hardened human heart,—if he can bring light to the eye or wholesome color to the faded cheek,—if he can bring or restore in ever so slight degree the sunshine of hope, of pleasure, of gayety,— surely he cannot have worked in vain."

III.

SOME ESSENTIALS OF THE ACTOR'S ART.

My friend Mr. Joseph Holland is a delightful walking demonstration of so much in the art of acting, that I hope he will allow me to put his name at the top of this essay as a pattern into which I may weave the threads of my discourse. If, when I stop work, the reader is unable clearly to distinguish the outlines of the figure, I am willing to have him believe that it is the fault of the weaver and not of the pattern.

Mr. Holland has the first requisite for the actor's art—sensibility, or an instinctive feeling for histrionic effects. Therefore is he a good actor without being a great one. Were he the latter he would have added to his sensibility an acute and vigorous intellectuality: he would not be playing this year in farce, however good, but in high comedy or in tragedy.

In all presentations of the actor's art, save the very highest, it is indeed temperament or sensibility which is most important. Many clever people have failed upon the stage and have found their failure utterly inexplicable, because they could not or would not recognize this basal principle. On the other hand, many people of the most ordinary intellect have succeeded on the stage because they possessed this temperament or feeling. Such people, provided they are not absolutely stupid, can be taught to act just as anybody above the level of a *crétin* can be taught the elements of drawing and of carpentry. Thackeray saw this very clearly, and in the character of Miss Fotheringay has described, in his own inimitable manner, the process by which a person who possesses this temperament in even a slight degree may achieve stage success. In "Pendennis" he writes: "Bows * * * was a singular wild man of no small talents and humor. Attracted first by Miss Fotheringay's beauty, he began to teach her how to act. He shrieked out in his cracked voice the parts, and his pupil learned them from his lips by rote and repeated them in her full, rich tones. He indicated the attitudes and set and moved those beautiful arms of hers. Those who remember this grand actress on the stage can recall how she used always precisely the same gestures, looks and tones; how she stood on the same plank of the stage in the same position, rolled her eyes at the same instant and to the same degree, and wept with precisely the same heart-rending pathos and over the same pathetic syllable."

To turn from fiction to history, we see this same general principle illustrated in the case of the most prominent actress of our day, Sarah Bernhardt. Nearly twenty years ago Matthew Arnold wrote of her: "Temperament and quick intelligence, passion, nervous mobility, grace, smile, voice, charm, poetry—[she] has them all. One watches her with pleasure, with admiration, and yet not without a secret disquietude. Something is wanting, or at least not present in sufficient force; something which alone can secure and fix her administration of all the charming gifts which she has, can alone keep them fresh, keep them sincere, save them from perils by caprice, perils by mannerism.

That something is high intellectual power." The prophecy implied in these words has been remarkably fulfilled. Insincerity, caprice and mannerism have become more and more prominent in Sarah Bernhardt since those words were written. With her great natural gifts she can never sink to the level of the mediocre, but, lacking this "high intellectual power," she has never risen to the level of the great—of that Rachel, for instance, with whom Arnold compares her and of whom he says that "she began almost where Mlle. Sarah Bernhardt ends."

If temperament unaided by high intellectuality cannot make a great actor, neither can this be accomplished by high intellectuality unaided by the necessary temperament. Sir Henry Irving, it seems to me, is a proof of this: he is a man who has made himself what he is by sheer force of will and intellect unaided by any particular natural aptitude for his profession. Only in those rare cases where temperament and high intellect are united do we find really great artists; such were Garrick, Talma, Rachel and Booth; such an artist is Mr. Jefferson.

If we descend from these generals to particulars, to what may be called the minor requisites of the actor's art, we find in Mr. Holland a model which all young aspirants for stage honors would do well to study. In the first place, he possesses the rare art of Elocution, without which the actor's voice is but as the sounding brass and the tinkling cymbal. Nothing is more justly infuriating to an audience than to miss even a small portion of the dialogue upon the stage, yet the actors who can so speak as to make every word audible in every portion of the house are the exceptions and not the rule. This comes either from incapacity or from carelessness; if from the former, the actor should be retired to private life by his manager; if from the latter, it is entirely inexcusable and should not be tolerated by the audience. Such an actor in England or in Italy would be hissed off the stage; that he is not so treated in the United States is but another instance of that easy-going indifferentism which Mr. Herbert Spencer points out as among our national failings.

Next among the minor graces of the actor may be mentioned Repose, the objective manifestation of which is the Art of Standing Still. Easy as this may appear from the front, those on the stage know (or should know) that it is indeed difficult; it is an art by most actors more honored in the breach than in the observance. The reason for their common failure in this respect is evident. Acting, by its very name implies action, which leads the actor to forget that not all acting implies action. Many times in a play the interest needs to be centered upon the person speaking: these are the times when the other people on the stage need to cultivate the arts of listening and of standing still, yet how few of them do! But when done, how greatly this enhances the verisimilitude of the stage picture! Those who have seen Mr. McDowell in *Gismonda* as he stands listening to the impassioned speeches of the Duchess, will recognize what I mean. There are even occasions when, in the very torrent and tempest of passionate declamation, the actor who knows how to stand still can give an appearance of solidity and force to his work which cannot be achieved by one who has not mastered this art.

Sir Henry Irving has pointed out that a Bearing or Carriage suitable to the time in which the play is set is a not unimportant detail in the actor's art. "The free bearing of the sixteenth century," he says, "is distinct from the artificial one of the seventeenth, the mannered one of the eighteenth and the careless one of the nineteenth." This nineteenth century bearing Mr. Holland has, it seems to me, in perfection: his manner and tone are thoroughly easy and careless, yet never slipshod or vulgar. Nor is this easy bearing such an easy thing to acquire. Witness the case of Mr. Lucius Henderson, who, intelligent actor though he is, in playing a modern part similar to Mr. Holland's, makes the mistake of carrying it with the "free bearing of the sixteenth century."

Perfection, it has been well said, is made up of little things, but perfection is not a little thing.

IV.

THE ENDOWED THEATRE.

I.

There is little doubt that of recent years Shakespeare has been more appreciated as a playright in Germany than in England. Not many years ago one theatre in Berlin, the Koenigsliche Schauspielhaus,* during a short season of only four months, presented no less than four Shakespearean plays, the *Midsummer Night's Dream*, the *Winter's Tale*, *Hamlet*, *Othello*—the last-named frequently. In the year ending December 31, 1896, there were one hundred and thirty-five recorded performances of *Othello* in Germany, and this year an English company, headed by Mr. Forbes Robertson, is to play *Hamlet* and *Macbeth* in Hamburg, Munich, Frankfort, Han-

---

* For the Koenigsliche Schauspielhaus statistics. I am indebted to an article by Mr. Wm. Archer in the *Fortnightly Review*, Vol. 51, page 610.

over and Berlin. If this state of affairs does not entirely prove the modest claim of our German friends—that Shakespeare was a German—it may certainly afford them at least reasonable ground for their conviction that he ought to have been.

While the Germans have been engaged in acting Shakespeare, Shakespeare's own countrymen have been engaged principally in writing books about him—and such books! Most of them fully justify the despairing wail of one who exclaimed after wading through an extensive slough of Shakespearean commentaries: "If you would know the heights to which the human intellect can rise, read Shakespeare; if you would know the depths to which it can fall, read his commentators." To such an extreme has the pedantry of the English been carried that in many of their annotated editions of Shakespeare the notes actually occupy more space than the text, and it is through the distorting medium of these notes that the feeble vision of the young student is expected to pierce before he can see, face to face, the clearest and greatest mind of the poetic world. Some commentators, such as Mr. Andrew Lang, have even argued themselves into the ridiculous belief that the Shakespearean plays should never be acted, but simply be read. Only thus, they seem to think, can the supersensitive, ultra-refined, delicately attuned, critical mind (of the Lang type), only thus can it preserve intact ideal conceptions of Shakespearean characters; ideals which would be rudely shattered by seeing these characters embodied in such flesh and blood as Miss Ellen Terry.

Against this school of faddists and against the general apathy of the English people to their greatest dramatic writer, Sir Henry Irving has combated long and for many years single-handed. By means of gorgeous mountings and elaborate scenic effects the English people have actually had to be coaxed to come and see Shakespearean plays, while the same plays, mounted simply but sufficiently, were drawing steadily in Germany by the intrinsic merit of their characterization and their poetry. But the work done at the Lyceum in London during these long years is beginning to tell: gentlemen interested in art in the provincial cities of England have formed themselves into committees for the encouragement of the classical drama; they provide funds for this purpose and under their auspices some competent company is engaged to present Shakespearean plays at moderate prices. This plan has met with great success, Mr. Benson's company, for example, having recently played for two weeks in Glasgow to good houses, presenting *Hamlet*, *Twelfth Night*, *Henry V.*, *The Taming of the Shrew* and *Julius Cæsar*. Nor is the interest confined to the provinces. In London we have this year three carefully prepared Shakespearean revivals; the *Merchant of Venice* at the Lyceum, *Julius Cæsar* at Her Majesty's and *Much Ado About Nothing* at the St. James. The wave has reached even the universities. At Oxford, where, according to Mr. Churton Collins, there is a professorship of almost everything under the sun, except English literature,—at Oxford the Students' Dramatic Society has played *Romeo and Juliet* with considerable success for a whole week.

At last, then, the English are beginning to remove from themselves the reproach which I stated in the opening sentence of this article. They are educating their people up to an appreciation of the best that has been thought and done in the drama. They are doing this by the only means possible, that is, by regarding the drama seriously as a fine art, and not as a form of speculative investment which must be made to return fifteen or twenty per cent. upon the capital put in. This last-mentioned way of looking at the drama is the one prevalent in the United States; the first-mentioned way has long been prevalent in France and Germany. That is why the French and German theatres are so much better than ours, and when I say they are better, I mean that they present in better shape than do ours a larger number of plays that appeal to moral and intelligent people, that is, to the people whose hearts and brains keep the world a-going and the race advancing. This statement I shall now proceed to prove first for Germany, then for France. I shall then endeavor to show that it is possible for Americans no less than for Frenchmen and Germans to carry into successful practice a theory of the drama as a fine art as distinguished from the drama as a field for mercantile speculation.

First, as to Germany. In addition to the facts stated in the opening paragraph of this article, I would mention that in the same brief season and at the one Berlin theatre there referred to, there were also presented the following standard plays: Freytag's *Die Journalisten*, Heyse's *Colberg*, Lindau's *Tante Therese*, Calderon's *La Vide es Sueno*, Kleist's *Das Zerbrochne Krug*, Lessing's *Emilia Galotti* and *Minna von Barnhelm*, Schiller's *Wallenstein, Kabale und Liebe, Maria Stuart*, Goethe's *Egmont*. Is there any theatre in London or New York that can present such a record as this or anything approaching to it? I fear we must hide our diminished heads and sadly answer, No.

Now, this is not an exceptional record, nor is it a picked case; many other German cities can make a showing quite as creditable in proportion to their population. Some of these cities are much smaller than San Francisco; the little Saxon town of Halle, for instance, with a population less than one-third of ours, has a municipal theatre building which it is a delight to the eyes to behold and in which a well-organized company presents frequently the great classic plays of the German and the English stage. If we extend our view to the whole of Germany, we find that during the year 1896, there were performed twenty-three separate Shakespearean plays with a total of nearly a thousand representations. Had we at hand the figures for the Goethe, Lessing and Schiller performances, we may be sure that they would show equally remarkable results.

As to rendition, I will leave it to those who have seen performances at the endowed theatres of Halle, Munich and Berlin to say whether these performances are not decidedly more artistic than what one sees, with rare exceptions, in any New York theatre.

Any candid person who will look the facts squarely in the face will admit now, I believe, that I have proved for Germany the thesis with which I started—namely, that the German stage presents in better shape than does ours a larger number of plays that appeal to moral and intelligent people.

Turning now to France, I shall select, almost at random, the record of a month's performances—say, December last—at the two best Parisian theatres, the Comédie Française and the Odéon, and I shall compare this record with that of the performances during the same month at the two best San Francisco theatres, the Baldwin and the Columbia.

Among the forty-two performances given at the Comédie Française there were representations of the works of such excellent minor playwrights as Pailleron, Scribe and Erckman-Chatrian. Among the great writers we find, of the moderns, Dumas fils represented by four performances, at which were presented *L'Étrangère* and *L'Ami des Femmes;* Augier, five performances, at which were presented *Les Effrontés* and *Le Gendre de M. Poirier*. Among the French classic writers Racine comes first with six performances, two of *Les Plaideurs* and four of *Athalie*. Then comes Molière with four performances, three of *Les Femmes Savantes* and one of *L'Avare*. Of writers of the first rank, then, namely, Dumas fils, Augier, Racine, Molière, there were nineteen performances out of a total of forty-two; that is, nearly half the plays given were classics. A correspondingly good record for New York or San

Francisco theatres would have to read something like this: Bronson Howard, four performances; Goldsmith, five; Shakespeare, six; Sheridan, four. And even this is stretching the truth a bit in our favor. Let us look at the record of the Baldwin Theatre for the same month of December; it is brief and decisive: *In Gay New York* (author unknown), five performances; *The Jucklins* (Augustus Thomas), five performances.

This is the whole of the short, sad story. Let it stand there, monumentally, in all its sweet simplicity.

Lest it be claimed that the time covered by this record is too short to base a fair comparison on, I will state that I have made a list of every play given at the Française and at the Odéon during the four months, December, 1897, to April, 1898, and have compared this with the record of the San Francisco theatres mentioned above and of the two leading New York theatres (Daly's and The Empire). The publication of this list in detail would make us appear in no better light than we do above, but rather in a worse—if that be possible.

II.

In his attempt to account for the scarcity of good comedy in England, Mr. George Meredith divides society mainly into two classes. First, the Puritans or Agelasts, who will laugh at nothing and who never go to the theatre; second, the Bacchanalians, who are titillated by a wink and will laugh at anything. To neither of these classes does true comedy appeal, and as these two classes constitute a vast majority of English society, in that society comedy does not flourish.

If one might draw an inference from the plays presented at the San Francisco theatres during the week in which I write (April 17—24, 1898), one might believe that Mr. Meredith's analysis is as true of our society as of his. With the exception of the opera,—of which it is not my province here to speak,—there was certainly little or nothing to draw the Puritans to the theatre; or, to put it conversely, every play presented — *A Stranger in New York*, *Delmonico's at Six*, *The Strange Adventures of Miss Brown*, *Sinbad*—appealed only to the Bacchanalians, that is, to the people who can laugh at anything. Sympathizing with the latter class as little as I do with the former, I must confess that I find nothing in the plays above mentioned that is worth even the briefest critical notice. I shall, therefore, ask the reader to transport himself once more with me to Paris, where we shall consider the plays presented last December at the Odéon, and shall compare them with the plays given during the same month at our second theatre, the Columbia.

The Odéon is situated, as everyone knows, at the north-east corner of the Jardin du Luxembourg. Near it are the buildings of the École des Mines, the École de Médecine, the Sorbonne and the École Polytechnique. In this quarter of Paris, therefore, do students largely congregate, and this fact, for many years, affected the character of the performances given there. The educational authorities recognized and still recognize the immense educative force of the theatre, and the Government took care to see that a theatre largely patronized by students should include in its repertoire many standard classical dramas. Of recent years less supervision seems to have been exercised in this respect, and the Odéon has run more to modern plays, leaving the classics to the Comédie Française. Yet these modern plays are the best of their kind procurable. Richepin's *Le Chemineau*, for instance, of which there were twenty-three performances at the Odéon in December last, is a well-written, highly poetical, pastoral comedy, which would have been a dead failure on any English or American stage,—because poetical. Nor were the classic dramatists unrepresented at the Odéon during the time under consideration. Molière's *Le Sicilien ou l'Amour Peintre* was given twice; Racine's *Phèdre*, *Athalie*, *Les Plaideurs* twice each. Out of a total of thirty-seven performances, then, twenty-three were of a modern play quite as good as Henry Arthur Jones' *Masqueraders*, and eight were by Racine and Molière—a combination which represents to the French mind about what we express by the one word Shakespeare.

If we turn now to our home theatre, the Columbia, we find the following: Two performances of *Othello* and three of *Julius Cæsar;* sixteen of Hoyt's *A Milk-White Flag*, six brandishings of a dramatic crazy-quilt (by one Williams) called *A Cavalier of France*, one turning-on of the blood-bath yclept *Spartacus*, five rattlings of a child's kaleidoscope labeled *In Gay Coney Island*. If from this ill assorted heap we pick out the diamonds of Mr. William Shakespeare and the rhinestones of Mr. Charles Hoyt, I fear the rubbish that is left will not compare favorably with the finished work of Monsieur Jean Richepin.

There may be two ways of looking at the facts suggested by this comparison. One is to exclaim, as did Sir Sampson Legend, at the ingratitude of his son, "Body o' me, these things are unaccountable and unreasonable!" Another is to acknowledge that our practice is lamentably deficient and to try and find out upon what deficient theory this practice is based. Let us try the latter; the problem is not a difficult one, and is practically solved by the statement of it made in the first part of this article, namely, that the French regard the drama seriously as a fine art and as an educative force well worth the attention of the best minds in the community; we regard it merely as an amusement and abandon it as a field for speculation to those whose prime interest must be to get the largest possible return out of it. Now, you can treat sheep and wheat and corner-lots in this way with perfect reason and with entire success, because your dealings with these objects have very little effect upon human character and human motives; but when you come to treat a fine art such as painting or the drama in this way, you invariably degrade it; to make it pay you must make it appeal to the average moral sense and the average intellect. Now this average moral sense and this average intellect in our present state of civilization are low, and an art that appeals to them for support must necessarily be far from ideal.

Only by making your fine art, to some extent at least, independent of popular opinion and of popular approval, only thus can you expect that it will live and grow and develop into what it should be. Strange as it may seem, too, if you are careful to do this it will in the long run really pay—not 20 per cent on the investment, perhaps, but a thousandfold—in the elevating and refining influence it will exercise in the community.

Something of this kind has been dimly perceived by many Americans, and clearly by a few. These few are typified by the generous men and women who, within a few years, have given no less than eleven million dollars to found the University of Chicago. Their donation has gone into what is technically known in this country as higher education—that is, education by means of libraries and laboratories and professors. These donors have done nothing for the drama since they have not perceived, or have not realized, the tremendous educative power of that art. This has been perceived by the Germans and the French, whose governments subsidize their theatres on exactly the same principles as those on which they—and we—subsidize public schools.

Admirably as this plan of governmental subsidy works in Germany and in France, no rational being would advocate its adoption here. Even if desirable, it would for many reasons be impossible, and it is not desirable. Yet, before many years, I believe, the problem of organizing an endowed theatre will be forced upon us, and we may learn something beforehand by noticing at what cost and by what kind of an organization the French people have made their theatre the first in the world.

The site alone of the Grand Opera House in Paris cost ten and a half million francs; the building 35,600,000 francs. It receives from the government an annual subvention of 800,000 francs. The Théâtre Français receives annually 240,000 francs; the Odéon, 100,000; the Opéra Comique, 300,000; the Conservatoire and Succursales, 220,000. The provincial cities also contribute generously for a like purpose. From the latest statistics I have been able to obtain, I learn that the subvention at the Marseilles theatre is 220,000 francs; at Lyons, 250,000; while even such small cities as Toulouse and Lille contribute respectively 87,000 and 75,000 francs. France is not as rich a country, either absolutely or relatively, as the United States. If she can afford to do this much surely we can afford to do as much. But for my part I should be satisfied if we could make a start with one-half of what the French people pay to one theatre, the Comédie Française. That institution receives in round numbers $50,000 a year from the government; this at 5 per cent represents a capitalization of $1,000,000. Let some rich man who wishes to see the theatre what it should be in our community— let him give merely half a million for endowment, and he will do more good, I believe, with his money than he could in any other way.

To make such a theatre a success the first essential is a good organization, and in affecting this we should not need to go upon blind theories. The present organization of the Théâtre Français has been in successful operation for eighty-six years, and contains several features that could be incorporated in the plan of an American-endowed theatre. By the constitution of the Français the actors are divided into two classes, *sociétaires* and *pensionnaires*. The former only are stockholders and in addition to their salaries receive a certain percentage of the profits. The *pensionnaires* are younger and less experienced actors, who are serving their apprenticeship, and from their body the *sociétaires* are elected. At the end of ten years of service a *sociétaire* may be re-elected; at the end of 20 years' service he may retire with a moderate pension. If he be a distinguished artist, he has then no trouble in securing profitable engagements at other theatres, or he may become a professor in the Conservatoire, where the actors and actresses of the next generation enjoy the immense advantage of being taught by one who has devoted his life to the subject in hand. So long as this admirable plan is faithfully adhered to, France can never lack accomplished artists.

The Director of the Comédie Française is always a man distinguished in literature and for his knowledge of the stage. Such a man is the present Director, M. Jules Claretie. He is appointed by the Minister of Fine Arts. Together with six *sociétaires* and two *pensionnaires* he forms the administrative committee of the organization. While he has great weight in the matter of accepting new plays, his word is by no means law on this point, for he is assisted and largely controlled by a Reading Committee chosen from the actors and actresses.

Such is a very brief description of the

constitution of this famous company. It has an unbroken tradition of great writers and actors from the days of Molière down to our own; a tradition that embraces the names of Corneille, Racine, La Fontaine, La Sage, Voltaire, Marivaux, Beaumarchais, Diderot, Victor Hugo, Alfred de Musset, Augier and Dumas; Floridor, Madame Champmeslé, Baron, Adrienne Lecouvreur, Le Kaim, Mlle. Clairon, Talma, Mlle. Mars, Got, Rachel, Coquelin and Sarah Bernhardt. It has a magnificent library, and the foyer of its theatre is an art gallery adorned with statues and pictures of the great men and women whose names are indissolubly connected with its history. With such a tradition, with such a home, small wonder is it that the Comédie Française stands an object-lesson to the world, an exemplification of what the drama ought to be and might be in every large and wealthy community.

V.

THE FUTURE OF THE DRAMA.

Théophile Gautier says somewhere that the stage seldom gets hold of an idea until it has been worn threadbare in other places. This is largely true of the English stage to-day, but it was not always so and it need not be so in the future. The reasons for this a little consideration will reveal.

Those praisers of times past, who look back with unalloyd regret to the glories of Elizabethan days and who look forward with entire hopelessness to the budding promise of the future,—these people fail to realize, it seems to me, the conditions which made the seventeenth century drama so rich in eloquence and in poetry; they fail, also, to realize that these conditions have now given place to others greatly different, which, in their turn, we must believe, will give place to another and a better state of things a century or two hence.

The study of sociology shows us clearly that in all semi-civilized peoples the head of the state combines in himself the functions of leader-in-war, priest and medicine man. As the political organism becomes more complex these functions become differentiated and are discharged by separate officials. Now, just as the tribal chief in primitive times united in himself generalship, priesthood and therapeutics, so did the primitive drama of Elizabethan days unite in itself the arts of poetry and eloquence and the science, so far as there was a science, of history. What poetry, eloquence and history the common people then got hold of, they got chiefly through the drama: before the invention of the school textbook of history, the Shakespearean historical plays, from *King John* to *Henry VIII.*, offered something more than an equivalent; before parliamentary and congressional eloquence was hatched people heard real eloquence in such compositions as Antony's speeches in *Julius Cæsar;* before the time when degenerates like Whitman could get themselves printed and turned loose upon a suffering world, people had to get most of their poetry from such descriptive verse as the Queen Mab speech in *Romeo and Juliet*, and from such lyrics as "O, mistress mine, where are you roaming?"

Now, in the evolution of the drama, poetry, eloquence and history have become sharply differentiated; improvements in the art of printing have made it possible for these branches of human knowledge to grow to such immense proportions that the primitive dramatic form in which they were once encased has long been outworn. The children have deserted their mother, whom they now look down upon from an eminence of lofty intellectual and emotional superiority, to which they think she can never hope to climb. Stripped of her history—that is, her "philosophy teaching by experience"—stripped of her eloquence, stripped of her poetry, the drama is reduced to a mere skeleton of situations, and the art of play-writing has become little more than the art of constructing situations. Now, that branch of dramatic writing which depends for its effects chiefly upon situation is farce, and farce, if I mistake not, is the thing that most interests theatre-goers to-day.

Another set of considerations will bring us, I think, to the same conclusion. In Elizabethan times the stir and stress of life were not as feverish as they are now; competition was less keen, men were less eager after the material comforts of life and did not so often lose sight of the ends of existence through absorption in the means. When they went to the theatre then, they went with unjaded minds and a keen intellectual curiosity. To-day men go to the theatre fagged out with the rush and toil of eight or ten hours' hard work and suffering from the repletion of facts crammed down their throats by the thousand newspapers, books and magazines of the day. To a man thus wearied, the intellectual and emotional strain of following such a play as *Macbeth* or *Philaster* would be almost unendurable. He does not seek in the drama any serious food for thought or any high emotional effects; he seeks merely for amusement and relaxation: now, high comedy might amuse him if he were quick-witted enough to follow it, but it will hardly relax him, because it calls for close attention in the spectator; farce will both amuse and will relax his mental strain. Farces, therefore, or plays of a farcical type, are what he seeks.

Merely to provide amusement! Has the stage then really sunk to this? Is this the final step in the evolution of that noble art which can number among its practitioners such men as Sophocles, Shakespeare, Cervantes, Molière, Goethe and Hugo? I, for one, cannot believe it. I must believe that when men come to realize that railroads and factories and huge wheat crops and gold mines are not ends in themselves, but are only means to something better and higher, then they will spend less time and be less absorbed in those means and will demand that the drama shall graft into itself again those poetical and ethical elements which we see flourishing in the works of the great playwrights I have named. This change will hardly come in our day, and even our children's children may not see it; but come some day it surely will, if our civilization is ever to mean anything more than big prices for wheat and a perpetual boom in corner-lots.

II.

IMPRESSIONS.

I.

SHALL WE FORGIVE HER?— THE SERENADE.

(San Francisco, February, 1898.)

"Criticism," says Matthew Arnold, "is a disinterested endeavor to learn and propagate the best that is known and thought in the world." Now, the conditions of the acted drama are such that it is difficult —except at rare intervals—for the local critic and his public to attain to a sight of that "best that is known and thought in the [dramatic] world." For "the best" can seldom afford to travel three thousand miles across the continent, and merely to read about "the best" is as tantalizing as to think how many more good plays Shakespeare might have written had he not died at fifty-three.

Poor substitute for the delight of seeing, as reading must always be, yet by reading something may be accomplished. There are perhaps fifty plays in English

—the delight of past generations and the solace of this—the reading of which may tend to form in our minds a standard or model according to which such plays as we see to-day may be judged. If one be acquainted with French, this number of standard plays may be increased to a hundred and fifty. As to rendition, while one must confess that a thoroughly artistic play is a treat San Francisco enjoys much less often than we could wish, yet even in the way of rendition we have seen performances that make us realize how immensely effective is the actor's art when practiced by a master of the profession. Coquelin's Tartuffe and Miss Terry's Portia linger in my memory as never-to-be-forgotten ideals, while Miss Kidder's presentation of Madame Sans-Gene left nothing, so far as I could see, to be desired. Nay, in the days when we were in Mr. Frohman's good books, did did not the Empire Theatre Company, unshorn of any of its glory, pay us only too short a visit? And he who has seen Miss Allen and Mr. Faversham in *The Masqueraders*—that nineteenth century *School for Scandal*—he has an ideal for modern play-writing and modern acting to which he may nail his faith with justifiable confidence.

In the criticisms upon which I shall now venture, I shall presuppose upon the part of my readers some such desire for knowing "the best" as Arnold's definition implies, and as much acquaintance with this "best" as is indicated above. To such readers, the drama must appeal as a fine art, with a history, with an evolution, and with laws of its own. Such an art is worth studying and worth writing about. "The best that is known and thought" in this art to-day should challenge comparison with "the best that is known and thought" in any other art. When it fails to do this the failure should be pointed out; when it succeeds, the success should be generously applauded and the reason for it analyzed. In this manner may the critical faculty subserve the purposes of the creative faculty, blazing the path along which the creative genius of the future must travel if he would obtain to a Pisgah-view of the promised land of perfection.

Shall We Forgive Her? the English melodrama which Miss Wainwright has been presenting at the Columbia, is an excellent example of the dismal divorce which has taken place in English between literature and the drama. Here is a play which contains hardly a single thought—hardly an expression which rises above the commonplace. The language is not ungrammatical, and this is the only virtue one can ascribe to it; the thought is a second-rate recasting of Mr. Pinero's effort in *The Second Mrs. Tanqueray*. The construction follows that of Haddon Chambers' *Captain Swift*, the chief difference being that in this play we have a heroine, while in *Captain Swift* we have a hero. If the play were printed it would be as dull to read as is a page of Tupper's "Proverbial Philosophy"; not a shred of wit, humor or anything but surface observation of life does it show. Yet constructively the play is well made, with one or two ingenious incidents and a theme which, though well worn, must command interest so long as women are weak and men are cruel.

The success of this play, at such a theatre as the Adelphi in London, shows us that the questions presented in "problem plays" have begun to agitate the minds

of the middle classes of English society
and are no longer confined to those classes
by courtesy called "the upper." In order
to reach and stir the minds of this middle
class it is necessary, perhaps, to state the
problem in its most elementary form and
in the simplest, baldest language. This
is what the author has done. Nobody
can possibly mistake his meaning or the
answer which he would have us give to
the question asked by the title of his play.
No man with his heart in the right place,
if asked, Shall We Forgive Her? could
fail to answer "Yes"; in fact, the problem as thus presented is really so simple
as to be no problem at all. Any other
answer but "Yes" to such a question
would be impossible. When the curtain
falls you turn to your neighbor and say
with smug satisfaction, "Yes, of course
we forgive her," and you go home with
little more food for thought than if you
had been studying the multiplication
table. Now, had the question been stated,
Should We Forgive Her? here would have
been something to think about; something upon which to exercise a nice discrimination and something which might
make us doubt whether all is to be for-

given to a woman because she hath greatly loved. Here is precisely the weakest point in the treatment. The woman with a past, when justly reproached by the man she has deceived, does but iterate and reiterate "I am your wife." This is evidently intended by the author to be accepted as full justification for such concealment as that of which poor Tess of the D'Urbervilles was guilty toward Angel Claire. Such a justification one may well hesitate to accept, and in many minds, Should We Forgive Her? will be answered "No," rather than "Yes."

To descend now from generals to particulars, the strength of this play seems to me to lie in the first act and in the last, rather than in the third or climacteric, where one would expect it. The reasons for this are, briefly, as follows: In the first act the heroine stands out in sharp contrast to the surrounding characters; in the other acts she moves in a social atmosphere common to them and to her. In the fourth act the interest is shifted from the "eternal femininity" which has thus far dominated the piece and of whose monotonous weakness one gets somewhat tired—the interest, I say, is shifted from this and is concentrated upon the struggle going on in the soul of a man—a man much injured, much wronged, whose sense of justice struggles against his love. In these acts also—the first and fourth—the element of suspense is skilfully introduced and is thoroughly well managed. In the other acts, with the exception of the ingeniously caused disappearance of the villain in Act II. there is nothing one could not foresee after listening to the opening speeches.

As to the author's character-drawing, there is nothing calling for commendation outside of two minor personages, which owe their distinctiveness, perhaps, more to the skill of the actor than to that of the playwright. I refer to the characters of Jerry Blake, the miner, and Dr. McKerrow, the oculist, excellently rendered by Mr. T. C. Hamilton.

On approaching now this question of rendition, I realize that it is a most delicate subject to handle. Protest as will the critic, the actor may very naturally see in a criticism of his acting a criticism of his personality where none is intended. Yet the true artist will welcome sincere criticism if he be convinced it comes from one who, like himself, is engaged in "a disinterested endeavor to learn and propagate the best that is known and thought in the (dramatic) world."

Nothing could be better than Miss Wainwright's appearance and acting in the first act. Here, it seems to me, she was at her best, and the reason for this is simple. The situation had a touch of romance in it and was therefore better suited to her than were those in any acts that followed. Nature has endowed her with an appearance and a voice that fit her for a very much higher and more poetical form of play than an Adeplhi melodrama. Her peculiar field is the same as that in which Miss Marlowe has won her reputation—the realm of what Coleridge, for lack of a better name, called the Romantic Drama, and of which such plays as *Much Ado* and *As You Like It* are types. Such plays call for sensibility to poetic effects, lightness of touch, ease and grace of elocution. All of these qualities Miss Wainwright possesses, as those who have seen her *Rosalind* can well remember. In such plays and in high comedy, crude and violent emotions have little place; now, crude and violent emotions are the life and breath of melodrama.

The art of writing light opera has been practiced now for many years and experience has plainly demonstrated that there are only two ways in which anything worth calling an artistic success can be achieved in this particular line of work. The first is to invent or discover a probable and entertaining plot wherein the incidents shall be properly motived and the characters shall so act and react upon each other that we shall have that clash and conflict of interests which are essential to a play : in other words, construct your dialogue as carefully as you would for a comedy, then give the whole a musical setting by inserting songs and choruses where they will least hinder the action. This is the French method, to the careful handling of which we owe such artistic gems as *Olivette, Les Cloches de Corneville* and *Giroflé-Girofla*. The second method is to select some institution or fad or fashionable folly which you wish to satirize, turn into lyrical form your most humorous excogitations upon this basal theme and connect your lyrics as well as you can by means of dialogue, which by its wit shall atone for its lack of coherence. This is the common method in English operettas, and according to Mr. Gilbert's own confession it is the one which he employs. To it we owe such happy satire upon Æstheticism as we find in *Patience*, upon the Admiralty as we find in *Pinafore*, and upon the Army as we find in the *Pirates of Penzance*.

I fear me that the author of *The Serenade*, as a good American, must have thought it unpatriotic to learn anything from the practice of such authors as Halévy and Gilbert, for his operetta has nothing that can be called a plot nor has it any basal or dominating idea. It consists merely of a series of happenings—to call them incidents were to use too dignified a word—which allow certain excellent singers to stroll upon the stage, sometimes singly, sometimes in twos and threes, and there to lift up their voices in tones so mellifluous that they happily cause us to forget the words. Should any one unreasonably desire to know the meaning of any of the things he sees a-happening on the stage he must perforce refer to his libretto, where he will find the stage business carefully explained —a most necessary precaution. He will look in vain for lyrics and will find instead a series of unrhythmical, prosy lines, printed in the form usually reserved for verse. Witness the following, a somewhat favorable specimen :

> We can hear our own hearts beat
>   With a loud pit-pattering.
> Knees together quaking meet,
>   And our teeth are chattering.
> B-r-r-r-r. There's something there,
>   Ambushed thieves observe us.
> B-r-r-r. To breathe we do not dare,
>   We're extremely nervous.
> We may remark we are afraid
>   And wish that we at home had stayed.

Is it possible that these lines were written by any but a deaf man ?

The only attempt at wit in *The Serenade* is a number of atrocious puns, and there is but one really humorous situation—that in which the Duke, in mad pursuit of the hated serenader, comes upon an entire chorus of monks singing that, to him, hateful melody. But this one humorous situation cannot save the rest of the opera from being deadly dull.

The composer has succeeded far better than his librettist. The Serenade itself, the Angelus song and the Dream song are charming bits of composition.

II.

A SECRET WARRANT.

(Columbia Theatre, San Francisco, May, 1898.)

The only play of serious interest presented during the past week was *A Secret Warrant*, with Mr. Robert Mantell in the leading role. The method in which the play is worked out raises it a step above the melodrama; yet this virtue is little more than negative. Of the commonplace there is a depressing abundance: of the elevated which may redeem this commonplace there is but one element. This gains perhaps by contrast with the surrounding dreariness.

The element to which I refer is the conception of the character of Marguerite Bertrand. This is thoroughly human, sympathetic and convincing. The girl's love for the first gallant man she meets, her entire forgetfulness of self where he is concerned, her unwilling belief in his apparent faithlessness, the crumbling of this belief at the touch of his hand—all this appeals, and rightly, to the common heart which has not lost its faith and love and hope. It is a thousand pities that the author who could conceive such a character had not imagination enough to set it forth in truly poetic form. You can see and feel what he is trying to do, and you wish that he could express it better. It is just as Thackeray said of *The Stranger:* "In the midst of the balderdash [of expression] there runs that reality of love, children and forgiveness of wrong which will be listened to wherever it is preached and sets all the world sympathizing."

The first act is entirely lacking in suspensive interest. Long before the curtain falls you can foresee that the villain will insult the heroine, that the hero will return just in the nick of time and will knock him down. This is evident from the mechanical way in which the hero's exit is arranged: there is no reason for his going off when he does except that he must be off the stage before he can come on again to repulse the aforesaid villain. The second act is decidedly stronger and is the best in the play; it contains a charming love scene and an extremely effective climax. The third act falls away sadly; the main situation has been used a thousand times, and the climax is so weak that the curtain seems to fall before the scene is completed. A touch of resistance here on the part of the hero would have increased his danger, our sympathy for him and our corresponding joy at his final deliverance. The fourth act is too long. The one really good scene it contains—that of the *lettre-de-cachet*—to be effective should be introduced more quickly.

In the comedy scene of the first act Miss Knott was disappointing. Thanks to the stage manager, I suppose, she played this in a manner that can be described only as "giggly"—a manner about as inappropriate to the piece and character as can be imagined. Throughout this act, also, she wore a Three-Little-Girls-From-School expression of pained surprise at everybody and everything which was entirely overdone. She reminded you of what Charles Lamb said of Munden: "He stands wondering, among the commonplace materials of life, like primeval man with the sun and stars about him." In the emotional scenes of the later acts she showed decided improvement and a capacity for attaining real excellence in this line. Her faults are evidently due to bad teaching. If she aspire to be in the future anything more than she is to-day these faults must be remedied. They can be remedied by a year or two of hard work with some competent master in New York or Paris, and this is the only way in which they can be. Miss Julia Marlowe spent four years studying only six Shakespearian roles. Anybody who expects to rise, as she has done, must be as willing to learn as she was.

Nature has gifted Mr. Mantell with a fine figure, an expressive countenance and a voice over which he has less control than the audience could wish. For declamatory and tempestuous passages this voice is sufficient, but in passages that call for the expression of tenderness and pathos it is lacking in shading, in delicacy, in refinement. That so experienced an actor should be nervous seems almost incredible, yet in the first act his continual clutching at his blue ribbon indicated either nervousness or a mannerism that needs to be abated. In spite of these defects, in the scenes that call for serious and romantic action Mr. Mantell is effective—as effective, perhaps, as anyone on our stage to-day. It is in the comedy scenes that he fails, and fails woefully. This, too, not from any lack of intelligence, not from ignorance of what is the right thing to do, but from a deliberate attempt to play down (or, rather, up) to the gallery. This is especially noticeable and especially inartistic in the slipper scene of the first act;—that an accomplished man of the world, a man seasoned by years of service in camp and court, should be agitated as a schoolboy and awkward as a rustic at the thought of putting on a lady's slipper —this is indeed incredible.

"A second lover came ambling by—
  A timid lad with a frightened eye,
    And a color mantling highly;
He muttered the errand on which he'd come,
Then only chuckled and bit his thumb,
    And simpered, simpered shyly."

This was Mr. Mantell's attitude. It raised a laugh both in the thinking and in the unthinking portions of the audience, but that which inspired the laugh was not the same in both cases.

In the drinking scene of the last act Mr Mantell shows the same tendency to play down. There is some (but not sufficient) excuse for this here, as the action requires that De Beaumont should deceive De Varennes by pretending drunkenness. In this place Mr. Mantell would do well to change the action, which is not only stale and unnecessary, but even tends to weaken the scene. Since De Varennes is drunk and De Beaumont is not, the audience feels there is no credit for De Beaumont in vanquishing De Varennes in the duel: a sword contest between a drunken man and a sober one is too one-sided to be interesting. Let De Varennes be kept sober. This will remove any possible excuse for horse-play on the part of De Beaumont, and will, as I have said, strengthen the interest.

The atmosphere of the play, in the two scenes just spoken of, was thus spoiled by Mr. Mantell. Among others who failed to preserve this atmosphere the chief sinner was Mr. Harry Saint Maur. This excellent comedian has so long represented old men that are loudly humorous that he seems unable to transform himself when called upon to play a character that that is quietly witty, or at least intended to be so. The author, I must confess, though his intention is evident, has not given Mr. Saint Maur much assistance. I suggest that with Mr. Mantell's permission he strengthen his part by inserting a few really witty expressions such as he may easily cull from the maxims of La Rochefoucauld or the "Polite Conversation" of Swift.

It is pleasant to recall that at least two members of the company did admirably preserve the tone of the play and of the characters they represented. These were Mr. Howard Hall as Gaston de Varennes, and Mr. Frank W. Smith as Phillippe, Duc d'Orléans. The former was rollicking, dashing, yet always, even in his cups, the gentleman; the latter was dignified, impressive, and bore himself most royally. Mr. Smith has a face and figure that would admirably fit him to portray the character of General Washington. If ever the Father of His Country is put upon the stage successfully—and several attempts in this line have recently been made—Mr. Smith is the man to play the part.

With the exception of the costumes little attempt was made in this play, so far as I could see, to create an illusion that we were looking at a picture of life in the days of the Regency. Nineteenth century sofas stood out in bewildering contrast against Louis Quatorze walls, bringing home to the audience painful realization of a truth unnecessarily stated on the programme: that the furniture used was from a shop just around the corner. Fearful, too, was the English pronunciation of some of the minor characters, and more fearful their French!

The avoidable defects pointed out in this representation make one realize the necessity of some such institution as I have before advocated and still advocate: an endowed theatre with a school attached, where the actor shall be trained for his profession as thoroughly as are the lawyer, the doctor, the college professor, for theirs. Until we have some such institution we can hardly hope for performances much more artistic than those uneven representations given us by Mr. Mantell's company—representations where good material is misguided and wasted through lack of intelligent training in the higher details of the actor's art.

III.

ROBIN HOOD.

(*San Francisco, March, 1898.*)

As I look over the playbills for this week (March 19-26), I find that one can choose only between two crude melodramas and two pieces written solely to amuse. Now amusement, though far from the highest, is certainly a legitimate end for the drama, and the amusement offered shall therefore be my theme.

As to *Robin Hood*, to state the matter negatively, it may be said that one's enjoyment of this opera is greatly enhanced by not reading the libretto; positively, then, the chief interest lies in the music.

Orchestration can be taught to anybody with a good ear and enough brains to remember what he is taught; but melody comes by nature and the grace of inspiration. Now Mr. de Koven is a born melodist; like the lover in Keats' "Ode on a Grecian Urn," he is indeed a

> Happy melodist, unwearied,
> Forever piping songs—

Alas! that we cannot truthfully apply to his songs the closing words of Keats' line,—[songs] "forever new."

Robin Hood is the one work in which Mr. De Koven seems to have given complete and beautiful expression to the musical thought within his soul. Everything that he wrote before *Robin Hood* is crude and juvenile; nearly everything that he has written since (in the way of operatic music) is commonplace or repetitional. His one great success came to him too early in life; it came, evidently, before he had realized the responsibility which rests upon that one man in a hundred million who possesses the divine gift of melodious expression. Such a talent should be sedulously nourished and sparingly used. It should be increased by assiduous study of the best models and should be strengthened by innumerable exercises which should never reach the ear of the public. Only in this way can great results be attained. He who would share the fame of a Mozart or a Beethoven must model his practice upon theirs.

Mr. De Koven has, unfortunately for his musical reputation, preferred money to fame. Had he given us but one opera every three or four years, each one of these might have been a masterpiece, as is *Robin Hood*. Instead of this, he has averaged at least one opera a year since 1890; who that has sat through the inanities of his *Fencing Master* and other tenth-rate work of that character, but must regret the squandering of a talent well worthy of being husbanded!

The popularity of *Robin Hood*, then, is, in my opinion, due chiefly to the life and grace of its melodies; yet there are minor elements in its phenomenal success which may be worth noticing. The theme and the setting are certainly well chosen. "*Orsino*, by Mr. Barrymore—What a full Skakespearian sound it carries!" says Charles Lamb. Similarly, what associations of the merry greenwood and the jovial outlaws cling around the names of Robin Hood and Allan-a-Dale! To the German or to the French element in our population this will hardly appeal, but to all those in whose veins runs Saxon blood, to those whose youthful imaginations have been nourished upon "Ivanhoe," to those in whose ears echoes the sound of old ballads :

When shaws beene sheene, and shradds full fayre,
And leaves both large and longe,
Itt is merrye walking in the fayre forrest
To heare the small birdes songe.

The woodwheele sang, and would not cease,
Sitting upon the spraye,
Soe lowde, he awakened Robin Hood,
In the greenwood where he lay,—

to all such the name of *Robin Hood* must ever be one to conjure with.

The story and the characters here are so well-known to the audience beforehand that little invention is necessary to carry them along. The only character in which any originality is displayed is in that of the Sheriff, and what would that be without Mr. Barnabee? *A priori*, it would seem impossible to extract any fun from the stale and vulgar device of representing an old man as intoxicated, yet such is the skill of this delightful actor that one can really watch with interest the contrast between his self-sufficient wisdom and his foolish actions. It is only after you go home and think it all over that you regret that such skill should be displayed in so unworthy a situation.

Nothing could better illustrate the doggerel which the public will endure in opera than the words of the famous introduced song, "Oh, Promise Me." Here is the first verse of this extraordinary farrago:

Oh, promise me that some day you and I
    Will take our love together to some sky
Where we can be alone, and faith renew,
    And find the hollows where those flowers grew.
The first sweet violets of early spring,
    That come in whispers, fill our thoughts,
And sing of love unspeakable that is to be.
    Oh, promise me, oh, promise me.

Compare this with the treatment of the contrasting emotion by a great artist:

Dear as remembered kisses after death,
And sweet as those by hopeless fancy feign'd
On lips that are for others; deep as love,
Deep as first love, and wild with all regret;
O Death in Life, the days that are no more.

IV.

THE GEISHA—RIP VAN WINKLE (OPERA)—A GILDED FOOL.

(*San Francisco, March, 1898.*)

Why has the English-speaking race, which has accomplished so much in all forms of poetry, accomplished so little in the other fine arts of painting, sculpture and, above all, music? Anything like a complete answer to this question would fill more pages than are contained in this book, yet a brief consideration of historical causes may throw a little light upon the subject.

Before the days of Puritan ascendancy the English and the Flemish schools of music were as strong and as original as any in Europe. In proof of this, for England suffice it to mention the names of Tallis, Byrd and Orlande Gibbons, all of whom died before 1626. The works of the first-mentioned still serve as models for composers of church music, while the madrigals of Byrd and Gibbons are hardly surpassed by those of Sir Arthur Sullivan. The glorious summer of English music, which ended with the death of Gibbons in 1625, was followed by the cruel winter of Puritan discontent. Though the educated among the Puritans, such as Milton and Cromwell, were able to disassociate music from its use with the service of the church, the great mass of the people were unable to do this; to them, music meant ever ritual and liturgy. Now, ritual and liturgy they were determined to stamp out at any cost. And they did.

In the second part of the seventeenth century we find but one great musical composer—Purcell. He died in 1695 at the early age of thirty-seven and left no successors—for the vast majority of the nation was still Puritan and had no more love for music than it had for that brilliant and immoral Restoration comedy which drove the Puritan from the theatre. Under the early Hanoverians matters were still worse; the little patronage which music had received from the court was entirely withdrawn by monarchs who confessed themselves unable to see anything even in "bainting and boetry," as they phrased it, so that neither from the mass of the nation below nor from the ruling classes above could the unfortunate musician expect anything but neglect and contempt. As Puritanism gradually lost force, and when musical taste began to revive in England, no native composers arose to supply the demand. English music became the thrall of German and Italian masters, and a thrall it has remained until very recently. The great mass of the English people have not yet awakened to the importance of music as a civilizing agency. Until they do England can hardly expect to develop a composer that shall be to her what Wagner is to Germany and Gounod to France.

What is true of old England is true of new America. Our best music must long continue to come from France, Germany and Italy—for Dr. Damrosch's idea that a national American music may be developed from negro melody seems to me worthy of being regarded as the joke of the century.

The poverty of ideas which still characterizes English music is nowhere more painfully apparent than in music written for the stage. England has but one master in this line of work—Sir Arthur Sullivan—and the other composers try to copy him. Witness that musical farce (not comedy), *The Geisha*. In this production we have a second-rate attempt to imitate Sullivan's manner, with an entire absence of that individuality which marks his work as unique. The composer seems capable of better things, but he has been compelled by the construction of the farce to write a mere succession of ditties wherein the jingle and blare of the music hall are painfully apparent.

In the libretto of *The Geisha* (happily not printed) we see the same imitativeness which characterizes the music. Its prototype, of course, is Gilbert's *Mikado*, and the one distinct character in the play —the Marquis Imari—is a transcript of Poo-Bah, minus his wit. The one original conception in *The Geisha* is the introduction of foreign and native elements into the same play. This gives a chance for picturesque contrasts in setting and costuming, and this chance is well utilized.

Vulgarity is not a necessary concomitant of comic opera, as Mr. Gilbert's practice abundantly shows. He has also demonstrated that witty and even poetical elements may be effectively introduced. Now *The Geisha* has neither wit nor poetry, but abounds in vulgarity. The depiction of Japanese life is bad enough, but its coarseness is partially concealed from the audience by their ignorance of Japanese morals and customs. When we come to the English side we are shown characters that are supposed to represent English ladies and gentlemen. But the gentlemen—officers in Her Majesty's navy—act and talk like fo'castle hands off on a spree; while the heroine—wealthy and of good family—is endowed with the manners of a Spiers & Pond barmaid. Such a representation is bad art as well as bad morals. Sir Joseph Porter is intensely humorous, yet always a gentleman; Little Buttercup, though only a bumboat woman, does not offend with the Billingsgate manners of the English heroine in *The Geisha*.

He attempts a dangerous task who tries to do over again a thing already once well done. To such a risk have Mr.

Jordan and Mr. Barnabee exposed themselves by offering to the puplic another musical version of *Rip Van Winkle*. The music of the first named suffers by comparison with that of Planquette; it is lacking in distinctiveness and melody, is full of repetitions and commonplace cadences that remind one of " Darling I am Growing Old " and other favorites of the organ-grinder. The libretto is even weaker and more pitiably amateurish than the music. It is—like to Mr. Clayton Hooper in *The Rival Curates*—the mildest thing a-going; to write such a libretto the author must have gone through a course of training like unto Mr. Hooper's, who

> Lived on curds and whey,
>   And daily sang their praises,
> And then he'd go and play
>   With buttercups and daisies.

As to Mr. Barnabee's acting, it is no discourtesy to him to say that he is not a Jefferson. Neither is it his fault that he is left lying on the stage for twenty-five minutes, during which there is being performed music certainly well calculated to put him to sleep were he not already so. Mrs. Siddons during a shorter period of enforced inactivity on the stage used to refresh herself from a pint of porter placed behind a (painted) rock conveniently low; let us hope that Mr. Barnabee's apparent slumber was soothed by liquid ministrations conveyed to him through some concealed piping, conveniently long.

Mr. Belasco's attempt at the Alcazar to establish a permanent stock company in San Francisco is a step in the right direction. It would be gratifying to see this attempt receive from the public a more generous support. Only by recognition of such efforts will the pernicious star system be discouraged, and in stock companies only, can the young actor acquire that varied experience which shall make him an artist.

If we except *Robin Hood*—which everybody by this time may be supposed to have seen—the Alcazar revival of Henry Guy Carleton's *A Gilded Fool* was the most enjoyable performance given at any San Francisco theatre last week. Here we had a play—a natural and probable story of human life presented by means of action and dialogue, through a series of properly motived incidents. Nothing in the play is irrational or improbable, which is more than can be said, I think, for the majority of plays one sees nowadays. Moreover, this play is actually based upon an idea and has a decided ethical tendency. Its purpose is to show how the nature of a man once strong and true but now weakened and warped by the acquisition of sudden wealth, may be restrengthened and revivified by the touch of some ennobling emotion; this emotion is love for a good woman. Innumerable poets and playwrights have treated this theme under different aspects—among others, Dryden most beautifully in his *Cymon and Iphigenia*. Mr. Carleton has given the subject a thoroughly modern setting and thus translated it into terms familiar to nineteenth century hearers. Wonderful to relate, also, he has managed to keep some of the poetic elements which many managers assure us that modern audiences will not tolerate. I was interested to notice that no passages were listened to with more attention than those which, to use Ruskin's definition of poetry, suggested noble grounds for the noble emotions.

The presentation of the play, though in

many ways excellent, was impaired by undue haste and insufficiency of rehearsal. This is unfortunately almost unavoidable at a house where a different play has to be presented every week in order to attract the public. Were the patronage better, were it as good as it should be in a city of the size of San Francisco, such a play as *A Gilded Fool* could run two—perhaps three—weeks. This would give time for fifteen or twenty rehearsals of the next play, and these would be none too many. At the Comédie Française twenty-five or thirty rehearsals are common, and forty or fifty are not unknown. The result is a finish and a perfection in detail which can be appreciated only when seen.

Mr. Pascoe, Mr. Huntington and Mr. Bryant are all excellent actors. Were they but allowed time fully to prepare their work they would fill every requirement which the spectator may reasonably demand from members of a stock company.

V.

THE CAT AND THE CHERUB—THE FIRST BORN—A GAY DECEIVER.

(*San Francisco, April, 1898.*)

The appearance of *The Cat and The Cherub* at the Baldwin may properly mark the close of one of the most exciting and most amusing controversies in the history of the American drama. The pother all started in San Francisco; in San Francisco, with dramatic propriety, it ends. Now that the fuss is all over, now that the clouds of dust raised by the friends of Mr. Fernald and of Mr. Powers have been nearly blown away, now it may be possible to get a clear view of the situation and to draw up a last and impartial report upon this famous battle of authors and managers.

Mr. Fernald's stories of Chinese life had been published in New York and had been well known in San Francisco many months before *The First Born* had its first rehearsal. *A priori*, it seems impossible that a California author contemplating a play upon a Chinese subject should have failed to acquaint himself with these vivid sketches. When we come to examine the elements of Mr. Powers' play we find that many of them are the same as those in Mr. Fernald's stories. Just as the theme of *Othello* is jealousy and of *Macbeth* ambition, so the theme of *The First Born* is parental affection. Now, this is also the theme in the narrative version of *The Cat and The Cherub*. The adventure which befell Hoo Chee could never have befallen him had it not been for the situation in which he was placed by the jealous love of his father. The plot of *The First Born* turns upon exactly the same motive. Coming to characters, we find other resemblances between *The First Born* and the Fernald stories. The learned doctor, the amah, the pipe-smoking murderer and the highbinders are in both; likewise the enmity of the clans, which furnishes much of the action of *The First Born*, appears in the stories. The pathetic episode of the slave girl is original with *The First Born*, and for this Mr. Powers is entitled to full credit, but for the other characters, for much of the action and for the color and atmosphere of his play, it seems to me, he is indebted to Mr. Fernald's book.

Had this acknowledgment been made at the first there need have been no controversy, no charges of plagiarism, no recriminations, and after this acknowledgment there would still have remained large praise for Mr. Powers. His originality consists in this: he was the first to perceive and actually to put into theatrical shape the dramatic possibilities of the life depicted in *The Cat and The Cherub* stories. So far as we can judge from the known facts, Mr. Fernald did not perceive the dramatic possibilities in his own narrative work until the success of Mr. Powers' play had demonstrated them to him. When these were brought to his notice we can hardly blame him for wishing to dramatize his own book. Our only regret is that he should have descended into the arena of music-hall politics, allowing his manager to exploit his play by unworthy dodges and tricks of the trade. If *The Cat and The Cherub* is a better play than *The First Born* it does not need to fear its rival: these mountings in hot haste, these hurryings to and fro will not make it a better play; they simply tend to keep away from the representations people who think that one of the essentials of the best dramatic art is dignity.

Is *The Cat and The Cherub* a better play than *The First Born*? To this I answer No; and my reasons are briefly as follows: The action of *The Cat and The Cherub* is slow; the action of *The First Born* is rapid; the dialogue of *The Cat and The Cherub* abounds in monologues, while that of *The First Born* is well broken and distributed. In *The Cat and The Cherub* there are really two stories between which the interest of the audience is divided; in *The First Born* this interest is centered and unified about one theme, and one only. The climacteric situation (which is the same in both plays) in *The Cat and The Cherub* is treated with tedious lengthiness; in *The First Born* this same situation comes with the force, vividness and unexpectedness of lightning-stroke from summer sky.

The treatment of this last point is another illustration of a fact familiar to any one acquainted with stagecraft, namely, that a man may write a very good narrative and be much less competent to put it into dramatic form than a man who could never have written the narrative but who has stage experience. Macready could never have written *Richelieu*, but *Richelieu* would never have been a successful play had not Macready been consulted at every important turn in its construction. Mr. Paul Potter could never have written *Trilby*, but he has put it into excellent dramatic shape. Similarly, Mr. Powers has done nothing to make us believe that he could write such charming narrative sketches as we find in Mr. Fernald's book, but his experience as an actor has enabled him to make a much better play out of this same book.

There is a belief current among people who cannot carefully have studied the facts that there is something in the actor's profession which militates against his being a good playwright. Among others, my friend Mr. Birrell holds this view and asks some one to point out what actor has ever enriched the literature of his own profession. To this I would reply, first, that Shakespeare was an actor, and that one reason why he wrote such good plays was that he had learned on the boards the technique of his trade; second, it was exactly the same with Molière. Farquhar was an actor before he was a playwright; so were Garrick, Foote and Pinero. This is a very respectable list of names. Some of these men combined acting and play-writing as long as they lived, and if others abandoned the former for the latter, it was not because the first-mentioned art unfitted them for the second, but simply because they found they had more talent for the second than for the first.

This knowledge of stagecraft must be acquired somehow. Congreve learned it second-hand from Dryden, Goldsmith from Garrick, Sheridan from his father (an actor). Each one of these writers would have learned it quicker and better from his own observation on the stage. This is where Mr. Powers has learned it; Mr. Fernald has yet to learn it—and I believe he will.

When we come to rendition, Mr Fernald's play suffers by comparison with Mr. Powers'. The actors in the former, excellently as they had acquitted themselves in the preceding farce, failed to adapt themselves to the tone and atmosphere of a Chinese play. In seeking for dignity they became cold and stilted; in bearing, gesture and manner they lacked verisimilitude. With the exception of Mr. Holland and Miss Deane, it was impossible to imagine that we saw upon the stage Chinese men and women. They were too evidently foreigners masquerading in Chinese garments. In the *First Born* the illusion was complete. Miss Buckley, Mr. Benreimo and Mr. Osborne sunk their personalities absolutely in the characters they represented.

Another circumstance unfortunate for Mr. Fernald is the position of his play on the programme. By half-past 10 people are tired; moreover, two hours spent in the atmosphere of the vaudeville and the *café chantant* leave one in anything but the proper frame of mind for tragedy.

As to this same preceding farce, *A Gay Deceiver*, it is excellently played and abominably written. In modern plays of a light order it is too often the case that the actor, by his interpolations and business, degrades the author; in this play the reverse is the case; the authors degrade the actor.

The theme of the play holds up to ridicule an institution which it has taken the human race thousands of years to establish on anything like a stable foundation. This institution is the most valuable which any society can possess. It is the corner-stone upon which rest all decent social relations. If this corner-stone were destroyed modern society would rush headlong to ruin and would crumble into a state of primitive anarchy. This institution is marriage; upon this rests the home, the family and the legitimate inheritance of property. To her insistence upon the sancitity of this institution ancient Rome owed much of her stability and much of her greatness. History shows very plainly that the society in which this institution has become a public jest is in a perilous condition. Such was society in the time of Charles II; such was society in the time of Louis XV; such is the society depicted in *A Gay Deceiver*. The men are all rakes and liars; the women are all shameless and vicious except the wife who is represented as a fool ; the authors heap the ridicule upon her—the only woman in the play with any pretension to virtue—and do their best to excite your sympathy for her husband, the arch-rake and the arch-liar. The latter's speech invoking the "memory of our sainted mother" is a slur upon a feeling which honorable men hold most sacred, and is an insult to every honest woman in the audience.

For these reasons I say the play is thoroughly immoral and is a disgrace to the stage.

I am informed on what I believe to be good authority that the play above described is an adaptation from the French, although there is nothing on the bill to show it. If this be so one may pertinently ask why (as in this case) American audiences will so often accept the offscourings of Parisian gutters, and will so seldom ask for the roses that grow in the gardens of fair France. French society, like every other society, contains bad elements, but it is an injustice to the French people to transfer to a foreign stage innumerable representations of those elements and to leave almost unrepresented those better elements reflected in the works of the great French dramatic writers. Paris has several theatres where such a play as *A Gay Deceiver* might have been running, say, during the first week of March; but she has also a Comédie Française and an Odéon where during that same week one could see the following plays: At the Française—Molière's *Le Mariage Forcé*, and *Le Bourgeois Gentilhomme*, Dumas' *L'Étrangère*; at the Odéon—*L'Arlesienne* (from Daudet's Neuma Roumestan) and *La Fille du Cid*. If *The Cat and The Cherub* needed a French prologue, why not give us something good rather than something vile? something elevating rather than something debasing? To use a Carylese metaphor: Is it believed that San Francisco has erected within her borders some huge signpost whereon is inscribed in letters so large that he who runs may read, "DRY RUBBISH SHOT HERE?"

VI.

SHORE ACRES.

(San Francisco, April, 1898.)

After all the foreign rubbish which has been shot upon our stage, it is refreshing to find a really good play upon an American subject, written by an American, excellently played by Americans in good United States suitable to the time and place of the action, and staged with a perfection of detail that would reflect credit upon any French or German production. Such a play is *Shore Acres.* If Mr. Augustin Daly and other high-toned individuals who think no production worth staging unless it has first received the stamp of London or Berlin approval, could give us anything as good as *Shore Acres,* their audiences would feel they had received full value for the two dollars extracted from oft-befooled pockets.

The main theme of the play is the devotion of a simple-minded New England farmer to a woman who is worthy and a brother who is unworthy of his love. In early life he had sacrificed his love for the woman in order that his brother might marry her. As an old man this long pent-up devotion flowed forth in a stream of blessing upon her children, and upon one of these (a girl) in particular. At the time the play opens she is supposed to be about eighteen. Her love story and the complications arising therefrom form the secondary theme or sub-plot. This, it will be seen, is thus organically connected with the main plot; each would be incomplete without the other. They are fitted together, it must be confessed, by the hand of a most skilful workman.

The first act and the third are, in my opinion, stronger than either the second or the fourth. The first contains an intellectual element lacking in the others. Its presentation of the narrow, provincial, country life of New England stands out in fine dramatic contrast with the wider, freer range of thought and feeling suggested by the mental tone of the young physician. The utter impossibility of life for him in a community whose most advanced thinker believes that Darwinism means that his grandfathers were monkeys; the hopeless attempt of the young scientist to adapt himself to such an environment; the faith of the young girl who longs to believe in the new ideas because he believes in them—all this furnishes a most interesting psychological problem, thoroughly modern and treated in a thoroughly modern way. This alone would serve to lift the play from the dead level of that ordinary nineteenth-century drama, which might be fittingly described in words I once heard applied to William Black's "Strange Adventures of a House Boat:" "Just the thing for a summer holiday; not an idea in it."

In the third act, to a good many people in the audience the strength seemed to lie in the spectacle of the painted ship upon the painted ocean. This bit of melodrama, it seemed to me, was out of keeping with the tone of the rest of the piece. It was really in the preceding scene of the same act that we had the most powerful situation in the whole play. Here was the real climax. Here we were shown, swiftly and vividly, the true nobility, the dauntless purpose which lay deep hidden in a nature apparently soft and sympathetic.

The fourth act—that terror to every dramatic writer, however skilful—opens delightfully in Mr. Herne's play with the episode of the children's Christmas Eve. It falls away as soon as the main action is taken up again and threatens to end in a perfectly mechanical resolution; it is saved, however, by one of those silent closes—so dangerous to attempt—so effective when successful, and never in my experience more effectively employed than here.

Turning now to rendition, I can hardly imagine how the principal part could have been played better than it was by Mr. Herne. Voice, gesture, bearing,—all were perfectly fitted to the character. Nobody in the audience could fail to hear every word he said, and when he did not speak his facial expression spoke clearer than words. Only in one incident during the long time he was on the stage did he fail, and that was in the struggle with his brother in the lighthouse. In a physical contest on the stage there should be enough action displayed by both combatants to create an illusion in the mind of the audience that what they see is actually a fight. Now, Mr. Fisher, who plays Martin Berry, is a big, strong man weighing over 200 pounds. Such a man with murder in his heart is not to be thrust aside by a blow that would hardly have budged a ten-year-old boy. The blow which Mr. Herne gave him in this terrific encounter would scarce have felled a six weeks' lamb. Therefore, when the audience should have been roused to terror and admiration, they were merely shaken by a very different emotion.

Next to Mr. Herne, or rather on a level with him, must I place the work of Mr. James T. Galloway as Joel Gates. Mr. Galloway plays the eccentric old man in a manner worthy of the best traditions of the French stage. Mezières himself could have taught him nothing.

The other minor parts are all admirably done, showing a thoroughness and an intelligence on the part of the stage manager (Mr. Herne himself) which is as rare as it is delightful. Here must be mentioned the clever work of the children, most of which, I suppose, must be ascribed to the same intelligent direction.

Shore Acres and *Little Lord Fauntleroy* are among the few plays I know of where the author's treatment of the child element is unobjectionable. In most plays (such as in that quintessence of vulgarity, *The Geisha*), the author endeavors to get a striking effect by representing the child as endowed with the "smartness" of a vicious man. An effect is thus obtained, but it is not really humorous or entertaining; it is rather pitiable and disgusting to see the fresh child-life thus polluted. This, the common type of stage-child, has been satirized by Mr. Gilbert in his ballad of "The Precocious Baby," who

<pre>
Early determined to marry and wive
          For better or worse
          With his elderly nurse,
Which the poor little boy didn't live to contrive.
          His health didn't thrive—
          No longer alive,
He died an enfeebled old dotard at five!
</pre>

Do we call this description satiric? No; it seems rather the model according to which many authors have fashioned their conceptions of stage children. While there is nothing of this kind in *Shore Acres*, while the child life there is really innocent and delightful, the question still remains whether it is good for the children themselves; whether it is right to subject any child to the late hours, constant traveling, and irregular habits which are the necessary drawbacks of the actor's life. In the growing frame of the child nature is ever working mysterious and subtle changes; she is making mighty draughts upon the vitality of the little organism. To place the child in those conditions which shall be most favorable to the growth and development of this organism is the first duty of those responsible for the child's existence. Now these favorable conditions cannot be obtained for a child whose life is on the stage, and for this reason the child had better not be there. If we must sacrifice something, it were better to sacrifice a passing effect in a play rather than the individual good of the young life.

The least pleasant thing to be said about this play I have reserved till the last, and were it a defect necessarily inherent and irremovable, I should place very little emphasis upon it. But *Shore Acres* is such a good play that it ought to be perfected in every detail possible, and the defect to which I refer can easily be remedied—from the front of the house it is so palpable, that it is passing strange it should have escaped the watchful eye of Mr. Herne upon the stage. I fear me that eye has been sicklied o'er with the pale cast of parental thought, for it cannot see what anyone else can see, that the cast of *Shore Acres* would be greatly improved by engaging a leading lady. The company as at present constituted has none. Miss Julie Herne makes an attempt at the part of Helen Berry, but it is only an attempt, and not a successful one. Owing to her youth and inexperience, or possibly to her embarrassment, she has not yet learned the art of standing gracefully upon the stage or of walking gracefully across it. In the earlier and quieter scenes of the play she was too slow and too drawling for even a country girl; in the later and more highly emotional scenes she failed to rise to the level which the situations called for. In a minor part Miss Herne would doubtless acquit herself creditably. With four or five more years' experience she may make a good leading lady. In her present role she has been placed in the false position of attempting a part beyond her years and present capacity. If we be told that the awkward pose and ungraceful walk are a part of the character, to this I reply that this is realism run mad and degenerating into detailism, or mere photographism. Photographism is slavish imitation of nature, and as such is not art. Art selects for emphasis from a multiplicity of details only those which are congruous with the situation in which the character is placed. The situation of Helen Berry requires that she inspire with love a man of taste and of refined feeling :—such a man could never love a girl whose pose is awkward and whose walk is ungraceful. If, therefore, Mr. Herne has deliberately taught the young lady these mannerisms I hope he will unteach her as quickly as possible, for I can assure him that the effect is anything but artistic.

Although Mr. Herne was for two years stage manager at the Baldwin Theatre, and although he has often visited California, neither he nor his work are as well known here as they should be. Those who wish to know something of his life in the old stock days should read his entertaining autobiography in the "Arena," Vol. VI, page 401; those who would like to know how *Shore Acres* came to be written should read his article in the same magazine, Vol. XV, page 61. I quote the concluding paragraph of the last-named article and rejoice to find it placing Mr. Herne on the side of those who have at heart the best interests of the theatre:

"It is generally held," writes Mr. Herne, "that the province of the drama is to amuse. I claim that it has a higher purpose—that its mission is to interest and instruct. It should not preach objectively, but it should teach subjectively; and so I stand for truth in the drama, because it is elemental, it gets to the bottom of a question. It strikes at unequal standards and unjust systems. It is as unyielding as it is honest. It is as tender as it is flexible. It has supreme faith in man. It believes that that which was good in the beginning cannot be bad at the end. It sets forth clearly that the concern of one is the concern of all. It stands for the higher development and thus for the individual liberty of the human race."

VII.

TRILBY—THE PURSER.

(*San Francisco, May, 1898.*)

In turning a novel into a play it is by no means important that the dramatizer should follow closely the details of the story. Indeed, it is seldom that he can profitably do so. All that the story can furnish him is a setting—a main incident upon which the plot revolves and suggestions for the principal characters. The minor incidents, the order in which these shall follow one another, the subordinate characters, the climaxes, the dramatic distribution of dialogue, the hints that prepare the audience for actions to follow, the *dénouement* and the best method of closing the play — all these must be worked up by the dramatizer with very little aid from the narrative. His task is fully as difficult as that of the author of the book—perhaps more so. As epic and dramatic faculty are seldom found in the same mind, there has grown up gradually a custom of collaboration in play-writing, where one author furnishes the setting, the main action and characters and the other author the other details mentioned above. In France, where the art of play-writing has been carried further than in any other country, collaboration is the rule and single authorship the exception. To collaboration we owe in French such masterpieces as *Le Gendre de M. Poirier* and *Madame Sans Gêne.* In English we owe to collaboration the two most successful plays of the last decade—*The Prisoner of Zenda* and *Trilby.*

Mr. Potter's dramatization of this famous story is now so well known that to point out the details of his method of construction would be indeed a work of supererogation : all I shall attempt to do, then, is to touch upon a few points which have not been brought forward prominently in any criticism that I have seen.

Mr. Frawley has a theory that what the public wants in plays just now is something that centers about a young and lovely woman, and this theory Mr. Potter has evidently worked upon in the opening lines of the first act of *Trilby.* The friendship between *The Three Musketeers of the Brush,* which in the book is fully as important and interesting as anything else, in the play is entirely subordinated to incidents based upon the young-and-lovely-woman-theory. This is somewhat of a shock to those who come to the play with the book fresh in mind; but before the play is ended you feel that in this case, at least, Mr. Frawley and Mr. Potter are right, both dramatically and from the box-office point of view. The interest excited in the young and lovely woman is never allowed to flag; it is consistently maintained through the four acts and ceases only when the curtain falls for the last time. In this respect the play is a model of construction.

The climax of each act is carefully led up to and is thoroughly effective, with the exception of the first. This is forced and miserably weak. Little Billee, shocked at Trilby's conduct, has strenuously resisted all entreaties of friends to stay in Paris and see her again. He leaves for Florence. He suddenly returns. But there is no reason for his returning, which did not exist before he left. His return is therefore unexplainable and is left unexplained. This is a dramatic absurdity, and one, moreover, that could easily have been avoided. Some accident, some stroke of fate might have been inserted to bring him back unexpectedly. The act could then have closed logically with a strong scene between him and Trilby, in which his love shall conquer his sense of duty.

The tableau which closes the last act is conceived and arranged with excellent taste. It would have been so easy and so entirely in accordance with stage traditions to spoil this by bringing on again the principal male characters of the play. Not to have done so, not to have broken in upon the sanctity of Trilby's death by the introduction of any but a woman friend, this is indeed a beautiful and poetic touch that thrills the heart.

Trilby would be a more pathetic and more human story if the hypnotic element were entirely omitted. Even the greatest masters of dramatic art have seldom succeeded in making credible the supersensuous. In Cymbeline, the apparition of Sicilius, the ghosts, and Jupiter upon an eagle are not credible; the ghost in *Hamlet* is barely credible; the witches in *Macbeth* are credible, but only because they are half human. Where Shakespeare has all but failed, we can hardly expect Mr. Potter to succeed. And he has not. Even in the book the hypnotic part of the story is weak and unnecessary. When put upon the stage its falsity comes out in glaring colors. Not even Mr. Paulding's art, admirable as it is, can tone it down to such shades as we may see in nature.

Mr. Potter has been careful to inform the public that he scorned delights and lived laborious days while reading ponderous tomes on hypnotism in order that he might present the phenomena thereof in truly scientific form. These days and nights, my Paul, were wasted. Your presentation of hypnotism might be worth a two-inch notice in the "Journal of the Society for Psychical Research"; but, scientifically, there is nothing in it, and dramatically, it verges on the farcical.

No one who has noticed the salacious turn given by Mr. Potter to the character of the Rev. Thomas Bagot need have been surprised at the outrageous tone of his last play, *The Conquerors* (happily a failure in London, by the way). There is nothing in Du Maurier's book to suggest what Mr. Potter shows us. Its introduction ruins the pure and wholesome tone of an otherwise pathetic scene, and all that is gained is an occasional cheap laugh from the lowest element in the house. I have met a great many English clergymen: none of them have ever shown the slightest resemblance to the creature conjured up by Mr. Potter's loathsome imagination. Mr. Charters did his best to soften the representation of the character, and for this he is entitled to the thanks of the audience.

Mr. Paulding's Svengali was an admirable piece of work. The character in itself is coarse and disagreeable; the only way in which it can be lifted from its low plane on to a level with the sympathy of the audience is by emphasizing the intellectual element—the sole redeeming feature in Svengali. This, Mr. Lackaye was never able to do. His rendition invariably made too prominent the baser side of the man. His death scene, in particular, was a piece of debasing realism quite as bad in its way as Hardy's description of the pig-killing in "Jude, the Obscure." Mr. Paulding makes this horrible scene less horrible, and throughout surrounds the character with an atmosphere of intellectuality through the medium of which we can suffer ourselves to gaze with interest upon a creation otherwise unendurable.

Miss Gillette is certainly the best Trilby I have ever seen. In tenderness, in grace, in strong yet artistically restrained emotion, she was decidedly superior to the best Trilby who has yet appeared on this coast.

The support was about evenly divided between good and indifferent. Among the good we must class the delightful Mme. Vinard of Miss Phosa McAllister, and the Gecko of Mr. Frank Clayton,—an excellent local actor of whom we have seen too little. Among the indifferent must come the three painters, all of whom, and especially Little Billee, were overweighted with their parts. The stage management was good and reflects credit upon Mr. George Lask.

In spite of some deficiencies, then, the performance on the whole was enjoyable. That a hastily collected local company can so creditably represent so difficult a play, is only another proof of what I have long firmly believed—that San Francisco is quite capable of producing in good shape, any play in the English language, and that the sooner we assert our independence and rally to the support of a good stock company, the better it will be for actors, audience and managers.

During the long years which Mr. Hartman was compelled to waste in stupid burlesque at the Tivoli, many who watched him must have felt that he had capacity to become something more than a mere caricaturist ; that, given the opportunity, he would prove himself an actor. Even in those dreary years, on the rare occasions when opportunity was offered him, he justified this belief by the manner in which he played such roles as that of Rip Van Winkle, of the Happy Father in *Giroflé-Girofla*, and of Gaspard in *Les Cloches de Corneville*. This last-mentioned part he was even able to invest with a tragic dignity which delighted but did not surprise those who had followed his career.

Mr. Hartman has now to be congratulated upon having taken the first step upon a path which shall lead him to a temple of more permanent fame than he could ever have hoped to reach as a player of burlesque. *The Purser* is not a remarkable play in any way, but it does contain some portrayal of human nature and gives Mr. Hartman a mild chance to display his excellent talent for representing the humorous side of things. Let us hope that his next play will be not less humorous, and will contain at least a trace of that intellectual interest which is the only guarantee of permanent success and an abiding reputation.

The stage effects in *The Purser* are thoroughly artistic, and there is some originality in the one really humorous scene of the play, that in which Mrs. Stanley is as fully convinced that Miss Somers is mad, as is Miss Somers that Mrs. Stanley is mad. How clever, too, was the acting of Miss Merville in this scene! The humorous portrayal of a woman's irrational fright could no further go.

VIII.
NIOBE—IN OLD JAPAN.
(*San Francisco. May, 1898.*)

No less an authority than Molière has assured us, that he who undertakes to make intelligent people laugh, undertakes a difficult task. A single stroke of humor, a single flash of wit, may be compassed at times even by ordinary people, but to be humorous or witty through a long narrative or play—and this is what Molière is referring to—this is indeed a task to be approached with fear and with trembling.

Now the process of being humorous, like every other mental process, is capable of being analyzed partially, if not with entire satisfaction. To go back to first principles, to the man of primitive times (represented by the savage of to-day) nothing is humorous. Everything about him is entirely so inexplicable by his weak faculties, that one phenomenon is to him hardly more inexplicable than another. Things that impress the civilized man as strange and incongruous, to the savage are neither strange nor incongruous, except so far as everything is so. As time—say a few tens of thousands of years—rolls rapidly on, man acquires, by bitter experience, the conceptions of cause and effect, of similarity, and dissimilarity, of congruity and incongruity. These conceptions are forced upon him by the study of nature and gradually they become hereditary in the race; for every effect the mind of man now instinctively demands an adequate cause; it expects that where within its experience certain effects have invariably followed certain causes, these effects will never appear without the precedent, adequate causes. On those occasions where the effect appears as the result of some cause not ordinarily associated with it, or when it appears apparently without cause—then, the mind, expecting one thing and getting another, receives a jar or shake of surprise; the physiological expression of this mental state is the nervo-muscular phenomenon known as laughter. To state it paradoxically, the ultimate aim and object, then, of a man who sets out to write a humorous play, is to produce, through the mental, this physiological phenomenon. This physiological phenomenon is pleasurable, or people would not pay 50 cents or $1 to experience it; on this psychologico-hedonistic-physiological phenomenon, then, rest the very existence and possibility of the Alcazar Theatre and of the excellent little company connected therewith. If this statement come with a shock of surprise to the energetic manager, I can say only that this very fact is another proof of the theory of the humorous here expounded.

If one ask the subtler question, why does the mental state above described manifest itself in the contraction of certain face and chest muscles, and not of others? to this I would say that although it is incomprehensible to us how nervous energy should generate feeling or *vice versa*, yet it is indubitable that there is a bond of connection between them. Emotion translates itself into nervous energy and nervous energy discharges itself (among other channels) through the muscles; why, in this particular case through particular muscles were too long here to be expounded. Those curious in such matters may find it clearly set forth in Mr. Herbert Spencer's essay on "The Physiology of Laughter."

Mais, revenons. Granting the incongruous as the largest (though not the sole) element in the humorous, it is evident that the writer who deliberately and with malice prepense sets out to be funny as before him two roads down which he may travel in his search for a subject. He may elbow his way along the broad avenue of the Commonplace which he will find crowded with men and women whose everyday actions seem to afford little material for humorous or poetic treatment; yet, if he be a real artist, his eye will often discern among these trivialities some little thing which, if treated seriously, may produce an effect at once humorous and moral. Such a method of treatment is difficult and is possible, as said before, only to a real artist. Such an artist is Boileau when writing *Le Lutrin;* such is Pope in the *Rape of the Lock,·* such is Gilbert in *Patience*.

If our searcher for humorous subject refer to climb up the steep incline of the

Elevated, he will find the path lined with many noble statues embodying some serious and affecting action. Any one of these statues he may trick out in the rags of the trivial and the ordinary: the effect is incongruous and sometimes (though by no means always) humorous. But the nobility of the statue is spoiled. Such a method of treatment is common and easy: by such a method have parodists ruined Longfellow's "Excelsior": by such a method have the Messrs. Paulton, in their *Niobe*, dragged down the beautiful story of Pygmalion and Galatea.

Yet it cannot be denied, as granted above, that the effect is often humorous on account of the sharp contrast between the methods of thought of artistic Greece as embodied in *Niobe* and of commercial New York as embodied in Peter Amos Dunn, President of the Universe Insurance Company. Admirably, too, was this contrast carried out by Miss Foster and by Mr. Stockwell; the former thoroughly pagan, dignified and statuesque; the latter thoroughly modern, ill at ease and fussy.

Outside of the two principal characters, *Niobe* is about as uninteresting a play as can well be imagined; it contains neither plot, wit, humor nor characterization. It is to be supposed that the society depicted in the play is not that of ladies and gentlemen, but of what Walter Bagehot would call "tenth-rate people striving to be ninth-rate people"; only on this supposition can we justify Mr. Huntington's talking of "photos" when he means "photographs" and his persistent fondness for making plural nouns agree with singular verbs. On the same supposition we must explain Miss Kingsley's entirely original pronunciation of the word "phonograph."

Considering the length of the play and the necessarily short time allowed for rehearsals, the production reflects credit upon that important and too little appreciated official, the stage manager (Mr. Charles Bryant).

As one looks at the pantomime one feels, How clever, yet how little worth doing! For the pantomime is interesting only as a *tour-de-force;* as an exhibition of what human beings can accomplish in histrionics when they voluntarily deprive themselves of the chief means of accomplishing it—the voice. It is as if a man should tie his feet together and yet succeed in getting over a hundred yards in twenty-five seconds. That would be a remarkable thing to do, yet decidedly not worth doing, for the free and graceful motion of the unimpeded runner would be a far more interesting exhibition of physical activities at their highest.

The pantomime, like music, suffers from vagueness and lack of definition. Like music, it suggests different things to different minds: it fails in unity of impression. As you look at *In Old Japan* you cannot possibly tell what the story is about unless you know the scenario. It might be about what Mr. Vance Thompson tells you; it might be about half a dozen other things; and even when you know the story many of the actions on the stage leave you with a puzzled feeling as to what they mean. Both Mlle. Pilar Morin and Mlle. Severine are good actresses and in the climax of the second act show a real tragic power. This power they are wasting upon a kind of performance that might appeal to the human race in its infancy, but which can hardly expect to hold the attention of men and women to-day.

The best thing about the performance was the accompanying music of M. Aimé Lachaume—admirably descriptive so far as music can be.

www.ingramcontent.com/pod-product-compliance
Lightning Source LLC
Chambersburg PA
CBHW031451160426
43195CB00010BB/931